HOW TO
PRAY

and change your world

david peters

HOW TO PRAY

Published by SpiritLife Ministries.
www.spiritlife.org.nz

Printed in New Zealand

Cover image by Hiroshi Watanabe via Getty Images

ACKNOWLEDGEMENTS

A number of people helped to proofread this manuscript, suggesting improvements, and checking the continuity of the writing. Their encouragement, and comments that the book was both easy to read and helpful to the reader, inspired me to keep writing.

Special thanks:
My precious wife Greta, who also envisioned the cover design.

Pastor Bruce and Diane Taylor.

Pastor Don James.

The team at McLaren-Brown Publishing: Anne McLaren, Paul Smith, and Pene Ashby.

Thank you all for believing that this book is an essential resource for our current times.

WHAT OTHERS ARE SAYING

David Peters has the remarkable gift of being able to demystify seemingly complex spiritual truths and open them up for everyone. In this accessible, practical and inspirational book, David invites us to turn our common experience of struggling with prayer into a transformed journey of fresh confidence, blessing and breakthrough.

— *Chris Cartwright, National Leader, Elim Pentecostal Churches, UK*

David Peters' book *How to Pray* gives clear, practical and inspiring insights, teaching you how to pray with simplicity and faith. If praying regularly has been a challenge for you, this book will help you greatly.

— *Joel Holm, Director, Pathfinders, Los Angeles, USA*

Why read a book on prayer? Because dialogue with your Creator begins the most profound and meaningful adventure of all. The experience of pathfinders such as David and Greta may provide the quickest preparation for your journey. These two have not just done their homework; they have lived their homework. Both have lived dramatic lives. They have overcome great suffering, born the weight of global leadership, and demonstrated true spiritual authority over many years. There are thousands of people like me who have been inspired and taught by David and Greta personally, but we have never had access to these treasures in a portable guide like this book. Put *How to Pray* near a Bible and begin to digest as much as you can until the big picture becomes clearer. Plunge into a conversation with God. You may need this book for what happens next.

— John Dawson, President Emeritus, Youth With A Mission International; Founder, International Reconciliation Coalition.

If there is one person who should write a book on prayer, it's David Peters. He lives and breathes prayer and has seen the fruit of this in many miraculous ways! This book is filled with practical wisdom that will take your prayer life to another level.

— Boyd Ratnaraja, National Leader, Elim Church of New Zealand

Overflowing with passion, wisdom, practical advice and guidance, *How to Pray – and Change your World* is guaranteed to "fire up" your prayer life. As you turn every page be prepared to sense the beautiful invitation of the Spirit to connect with your Heavenly Father in prayer and change your world! I thoroughly recommend it.

— Steve Ball, Regional Leader, Elim Churches, UK

David Peters has captured the true essence of what is needed to wake up a global Church that is losing its power and passion. The reader is constantly moved, both spiritually and emotionally, to pray. Not out of guilt or habit, but by God's heart for a world in trouble. I was very inspired by David's book. It's a timely topic and very powerfully written. It convicted me to take my praying to the next level. *How to Pray* will definitely inspire you to 'change your world'.

– *Malcolm McLeod, Senior Pastor, Equip Church International, Melbourne, Australia*

If you are looking for a book to inspire and equip believers to pray effective prayers that will change their world, I highly recommend this book. David writes with the clarity and practicality of a gifted bible teacher, the love of a pastor who is passionate about believers rising to their fullest God-given potential, and the prophetic insights of a minister who can discern the times we live in.

– *Vincent Lun, Senior Pastor, Kingdom Community Church, Singapore*

This wonderfully compelling and comprehensive book on prayer will enrich and empower every Christian, from those who are disciplined and focused in prayer, right through to beginners. It is so down-to-earth, but it clearly shows the way to intimacy with God, and opens the door to the supernatural and heavenly realms.

– *Adrienne Bhana, Senior Leader, Church Unlimited, NZ*

Whether you're intimidated by the idea of prayer, or you're a prayer warrior that commits hours a day, this book will help bring a revival of prayer in your heart and church for this time in history. Now is the time to move from self-focused to kingdom-focused prayer and *How to Pray – and Change Your World* gives you the why and how in a life-giving and grace-motivated way. A book for every person, every leader and every church.

– *Carl & Angela Crocker, Lead Pastors, Life Church, Christchurch, NZ*

David writes as a practitioner, a man who prays and who believes in the power of prayer. But he doesn't write in theoretical terms that can't be understood. He writes practically and inclusively, inviting all people into a lifestyle of dynamic life-changing prayer.

– *Duncan Clark, Senior Minister, Coventry Elim Church; National Leader, Elim, UK*

How to Pray is a book packed with teaching, inspiration and real-life stories. It does not shy away from the difficult subject of unanswered prayer, and helps the reader navigate those times of disappointment with integrity and understanding. This book makes prayer exciting, engaging and accessible and will energise you to join this powerful movement to change our world. Let it spark a revolution in your prayer life!

– *Rachel Hickson, Heartcry For Change, Oxford, UK*

David Peters has written a very important resource from years of practising the presence of God and from rich reflections on prayer. *How to Pray* addresses everyday areas related to prayer. You will find it readable and the stories relatable. This book will certainly encourage and equip you to grow deeper in your relationship with Abba Father.

    — *Ben KC Lee, Senior Pastor, RiverLife Church, Singapore*

Easy to read, inspiring, and very practical, *How to Pray* provides clarity and fresh insight on the subject of prayer. I recommend this book to anyone wanting to grow in prayer, from the seasoned prayer warrior to the believer struggling in their prayer life and desiring a change.

    — *James Aladiran, Founder, Prayer Storm, UK*

This is a practical, passionate and inspiring handbook on prayer for any follower of Christ. It comes from a heart devoted to intercession. A must-have resource for any Christian leader.

    — *Bruce Taylor, Asian Outreach International Network, Auckland, NZ*

What an incredible and profound Christian guide to learning how God wants us to pray. I thoroughly enjoyed reading it because the author, David Peters, beautifully explains each and every aspect of prayer. This book really helps the reader to clearly comprehend the type of prayer that will impact lives and change the world. I strongly recommend it to everyone.

    — *Gohar Bhatti, Evangelist, Lahore, Pakistan*

Throughout my life, I have always been inspired by practical teaching and testimonies of those who diligently seek our Lord and Saviour Jesus Christ. David Peters is a seasoned man of God, and in this book he beautifully explains the many levels of prayer and their relevancy in the 21st century. The testimonies he shares work well to reinforce the teaching, and allow the Holy Spirit to build our faith and develop our prayer life.

— *Bruce Monk, Apostolic Overseer, Equippers International and Acts Churches*

CONTENTS

FOREWORD

My name is Tak Bhana, Senior Pastor of Church Unlimited, and it's my privilege to provide the foreword to David's wonderful book on prayer. I am a great believer in prayer. I have always maintained that the church advances on its knees, and believe that this book has the potential to transform our prayer lives. Along with many wonderful faith building stories, it reveals a biblical pattern for prayer, practical hows and whys of prayer, and different forms of prayer.

When it comes to prayer, David walks the talk, or should I say he talks the walk? He is perfectly positioned to write about subjects such as praying prophetically, praying in tongues, engaging in spiritual warfare, and so on, because he and his wife Greta regularly conduct powerful and effective seminars on these very topics.

Let me share some stories from my prayer journey to whet your appetite. At fifty-nine years of age my father, who was a life-long Hindu, was diagnosed with a terminal kidney condition and given approximately three weeks to live.

Well, I was desperate, acutely aware that he was heading to a lost eternity, and highly motivated to pray more than ever before. I even fasted to add impact to my prayers.

My dad had never darkened a church door, and he did not appreciate me being a Christian, let alone going to Bible College. But in the end, through prayer and fasting, God graciously saved him. Through that powerful and personal miracle, I came to see that no one was beyond the reach of God's saving power and grace, and I also came to understand the power of prayer and fasting.

Jesus' disciples never asked him to teach them to preach, but in Luke 11:1 one of his disciples did ask him to teach them how to pray. David's book takes us through the Lord's answer to that request, and it's so helpful to have that pattern to guide us in our prayer times.

Prior to the outpouring of the Holy Spirit in the upper room on Pentecost Day, it looked like Jesus' mission was a colossal failure. Yet after the upper room, Christianity exploded, and changed the world. So, what was going on in that room that changed history? Acts 1:14 (NKJV) tells us, "These all continued with one accord in prayer and supplication." Here we see a prayer meeting of 120 people that changed history.

All the great Bible leaders drank from the ancient well of fervent prayer. This well of prayer is the one well that the devil hopes we will never re-dig or re-open in our generation. Well, the bad news for the devil is that prayer is rising across the globe.

It's been said, "The first revival in any genuine revival is a revival of prayer." Isn't that the truth, and may that be how it starts with each one of us.

Another powerful method of prayer is to speak to your mountain, as we read in Mark 11:23 (NKJV): "Whoever says to this mountain be removed and be cast into the sea, and does not doubt in his heart, but believes that those things he says will be done, he will have whatever he says." Three times in this verse we see the word *says*. We are to speak aloud to our mountains. Often when Jesus and the apostles prayed, it was more like commands such as: arise, be opened, take up your bed and walk, be cleansed, and come out. At times we need to stop pleading and start commanding.

Years ago, a neighbour right next to our church property disliked the church. So he would position speakers as close as he could to the boundary, and play loud music in order to disturb the services. At one stage a guest speaker came through, and God gave him Zechariah 4:7 (NKJV): "Who are you O great mountain? Before Zerubbabel you will become a plain with shouts of 'Grace, grace, to it.'" The speaker directed the congregation to face the property and shout, "Grace, grace, grace!" Not long after, the music stopped, then the property came up for sale. Church Unlimited now owns it.

Some time ago, I spoke at a church in Adelaide, Australia. I was told that the church wanted the building next door so that they could expand their capacity, and for future development. They had been desiring to buy that property for twenty-seven years. In the Friday evening meeting, I felt to get the congregation to stand and face the property and shout "grace, grace, grace" to it. The very next day the pastor had a contract for the purchase of the property.

I have also come to see the value of persistence in prayer. I believe that prayer is not answered at times because we don't persevere – we give up and stop praying. American pastor and author Mark Batterson shares a concept which I have adapted from baseball to cricket. Imagine a cricket player refusing to swing his bat because he doesn't hit runs every time the bowler bowls at him. He tries to hit the ball but often misses. We can be like that in prayer. We let our misses stop us swinging. My prayer batting average is not great – I swing and miss all the time. Everyday. But if I'm going down, then I'm going down swinging. No matter how many times a prayer is not answered, I keep swinging.

You might say, "I prayed for six months." I say, "Swing again." "But I prayed for two years." Swing again. Keep swinging, even when you have prayed for five years, ten, fifty – never stop swinging. My father was saved after approximately six weeks of prayer; my mother took twenty-six years. One of my brothers was saved after eighteen months, the next brother after forty years of prayer.

Truly our God hears and answers prayer. This wonderful book will help you become more effective in prayer and see more answers than you ever imagined. It's a must-have.

– Tak Bhana, Senior Leader, Church Unlimited, New Zealand

INTRODUCTION

The alarm is sounding.

"Pray!" cries the Holy Spirit to a slowly awakening global Church.

The world is in great need, with over 5.5 billion people living in spiritual darkness.[1] Before Jesus returns to earth, God the Father, wanting no one to perish, desires to usher in the greatest spiritual harvest of souls that history has seen. The keys to this are prayer and mission. But there is a problem.

Revivalist Leonard Ravenhill [2] put it best when he said, "We have many organisers, but few agonisers; many players, few prayers; many singers, few clingers; lots of pastors, few wrestlers; many fears, few tears; much fashion, little passion; many interferers, few intercessors; many writers, but few fighters.

---

[1]   World population in 2022 is over 7.9 billion including around 2.4 billion Christians, not all of whom will be true believers.
[2]   Leonard Ravenhill, 1907-1994

Failing here, we fail everywhere." (Or, succeeding here, we succeed everywhere.)

Prayer is powerful.

Prayer is our spiritual life breath.

Prayer is a means to intimacy with God.

Prayer creates a pathway of destiny for our children to walk on.

Prayer helps build a marriage, a business, a ministry.

Prayer opens doors of opportunity.

Prayer co-creates with God as he advances his kingdom on earth.

Prayer makes it easier for people to come to Christ.

Prayer, when answered, fills us with joy.

"Until now," said Jesus to his disciples, "you have not asked for anything in my name. Ask and you will receive, and your joy will be complete." [3] With an invitation like this, you would think that we would respond enthusiastically. Yet prayer is one of the hardest aspects of the Christian life to be consistent in, and the area that Satan will fight us in the most. Few subjects arouse a greater sense of guilt in our hearts than prayer.

_____

[3]   John 16:24 (NIV)

We know that we ought to pray; we know that we need to pray; and yet, the vast majority of us know that we don't pray to the level we should.

I can watch television for an hour effortlessly. To pray for an hour requires much more focus and discipline. I can read a magazine or be on the internet for half an hour, but to read my Bible for that time takes more effort, even though I know its words are so life-giving. Jesus revealed the reason why: "Watch and pray so that you will not fall into temptation. The spirit is willing, but the flesh is weak." [4] All agree that prayer is vital – our spirit is willing. But weak human nature often overcomes willing spirit.

There are three phases in becoming powerful in prayer: desire, discipline, and delight. The Holy Spirit gives us the desire to pray. It then takes discipline (overcoming the loud excuses of our weak flesh) to persist in prayer. If we do, prayer will ultimately become a delight. The problem is that we want to jump from desire to delight in one step. Discipline is the price we have to pay to get from desire to delight. When we get there, it will be worth it.

As a pastor friend once said, "Prayer is not a fringe activity, but the core business of the church. Prayer is both the price and doorway to the supernatural dimension." What lies on the other side of that doorway is worth sacrificing for. It is my hope that this book will help you discover an adventurous life of prayer, and its power to change a life, a family, a nation, and the world.

[4]   Mark 14:38 (NIV)

"Whenever God determines to do a great work," wrote great Victorian preacher Charles Spurgeon,[5] "he first sets his people to pray." As you read on, may the Holy Spirit do this for you.

---

[5]   Charles Spurgeon, 1834 - 1892

chapter one

WHY PRAY?

The story is told that during the Korean War of 1950-1953, an American soldier hid in a bunker during a battle. When his commanding officer ordered him to scramble closer to the front lines and rescue some of his wounded comrades, the soldier nodded his head. But then he glanced at his watch, stalled till the officer was out of sight, and simply made no move.

Several minutes went by, and a colleague reminded him of his assignment to rescue those who had fallen. Again he looked at his watch and delayed. Finally, he leaped out of the bunker and fearlessly began the risky process of carrying his comrades to safety. At the end of the day when the guns were now silent, a friend asked him why he kept looking at his watch when under orders to move.

Fighting off the tears, the soldier slowly raised his head and said, "I was afraid – because I knew I was not ready to die. I lingered for the moment when I knew my fear would be overcome, remembering that at a certain time every hour my mother said she would pray for me. As soon as that minute struck I knew I was under the shelter of her prayers, and that no matter what awaited me, I could face it." [1]

Such stories inspire us, and answer the question, "Why pray?" Yet we often struggle to pray. God's word commands us to pray constantly. "Never stop praying," [2] writes the apostle Paul. He also says, "Devote yourselves to prayer, with an alert mind and a thankful heart." [3] No doubt that soldier was very glad that his mother was devoted to prayer.

In the original Greek language of the New Testament, the word *devote* means to persist at, cling to, or continually be available for something. It was used in reference to boats that were constantly ready for service. They were not in dry dock being repaired. They were not up on the beach having their hulls cleaned. They were ready.

When crisis strikes, our readiness to pray our way through it will depend on how well we have cultivated a life of prayer in the normal rhythm of daily life. If we are devoted to prayer in good times, we will have the strength to pray in tough times. The Bible instructs us to be: "joyful in hope, patient in affliction, faithful in prayer." [4]

This scripture describes a sequence that we often see in life. God gives us hope, which is a confident expectation of

---

[1]   Adapted from *Deliver Us From Evil*, Dallas, Word Publishing, 1996, p. 158-159
[2]   1 Thessalonians 5:17
[3]   Colossians 4:2
[4]   Romans 12:12 (NIV)

future good. It's not too long, however, before hope-destroying affliction or satanic attack may come knocking on our door. But if we persevere in faith and constant prayer, then that hope will be eventually realised.

Two Mercies for Every Woe

My first wife Jane suffered from multiple sclerosis. Healthy and in remission when we first married, the disease progressed and confined her to a wheelchair for the last twenty-one years of her life. We continually prayed, not only for strength to endure, but also for a miracle of healing and freedom. I share the full story in my book *Hope*.[5] Many others prayed as well. But our prayers were not answered, at least not in the way we expected.

At the age of 56, Jane passed away due to complications from MS. At the time of her death, I prayed, "Lord, I don't understand this and am disappointed, but I trust you – that you are good and what you do is good. One day you will explain this to me and I am content to live with this mystery until then." Gradually, God healed me of the grief of her loss, and brought my beautiful new wife Greta – herself widowed two months after Jane died – into my life.

After marrying, we began a fulltime prophetic ministry which has taken us all over New Zealand and to a number of other nations. The passion to see people healed began to find expression in the Schools of the Supernatural that we run in many churches.

---

[5]   Available from our website www.spiritlife.org.nz or online bookstores.

Here we would teach on God's healing power and equip people to minister to the sick. After Jane died, I thought to myself, *all that prayer for her healing was for nothing.* As more and more people reported healing in our seminars and meetings, however, my attitude changed. "Don't waste all those prayers Lord," I asked. "Heal others from MS." To date, two women have been miraculously healed of multiple sclerosis.[6] Interestingly, both healings occurred in England, where Jane was from.

"There is yet hope," promises God through the prophet Zechariah. "I promise ...two mercies for every woe!" [7] *Two mercies for every woe.* God has literally fulfilled that in my life with respect to MS. No prayers are wasted if prayed with good intent. Though they may not be answered in the way we might desire, God will act on them. I am sure that all our years of praying for Jane's healing paved the way for these other healings to occur.

Greta's first husband Ron, though very fit, collapsed from a heart attack brought on by cardiovascular disease. Greta has since prayed for a number of people with heart disease and seen them restored. Whatever woe we go through, God will turn it to good, if we pray and ask him.

---

[6]   One of these women had many symptoms: incoordination, slow cognitive function, pain, fatigue, difficulty walking and was headed for a wheelchair. At a School of the Supernatural, someone prayed for her. As she returned to her seat, she noticed she was walking better. By the next day all the symptoms had disappeared, except the fatigue. As she kept praising the Lord for her healing, that disappeared too. When she met us, she had been symptom free for two years. The other woman was already using a wheelchair when she was healed.

[7]   Zechariah 9:12b (NLT 1996 version)

Disappointment Makes Us Sleepy

The reason I share the story above is that disappointment can destroy devotion to prayer. The night before he was crucified, Jesus prayed in one of his favourite locations – the Garden of Gethsemane. He took some of his disciples along, hoping that they would intercede with him. But they kept falling asleep. The Gospel of Luke gives an interesting insight as to why: "At last he stood up again and returned to the disciples, only to find them asleep, exhausted from grief. 'Why are you sleeping?' he asked them. 'Get up and pray, so that you will not give in to temptation.' " [8]

The disciples were weary, but not from a late night. They were *exhausted with grief.* At supper that evening, Jesus had told them that one of them would betray him to the Jewish leaders. They, in turn, would hand him to the Romans who would crucify him. Their world had collapsed in on them, and their hopes for a reigning Messiah dashed. Disappointment gave way to intense grief which robbed them of any strength to pray. Likewise, we can be weary not only from busyness, but also from the disappointment of unanswered prayer, tragedy, or adversity. And when we don't pray, we are asleep spiritually.

We Can Outgrow the Mountain

In 1924 a group of climbers on Mount Everest failed twice to get to the top of the world's highest mountain. In fact, two of their party were killed in the expedition.

---

[8]   Luke 22:45-46

They met in London afterwards to give a report. As the leader addressed the crowd, he turned to the picture of Mount Everest and said, "You have conquered us this time Mount Everest, but you will not conquer us every time. Because you Mount Everest can grow no larger, but we can." It took twenty-nine years, but in 1953, New Zealander Edmund Hilary and Sherpa Tenzing Norgay reached the 29,032-foot summit of Everest.

Disappointment need not be an unconquerable mountain that makes casualties of us or keeps us in its shadow. Start praying again in hope and enjoy the journey to the top, even if it takes a lifetime. In the words of the popular song *Rattle*:

> Friday's disappointment
> Is Sunday's empty tomb,
> Since when has impossible
> Ever stopped You. [9]

God is able to resurrect dead hopes for our lives, families, and nations. After every Good Friday there is a Resurrection Sunday – if we keep praying in faith. This is why we pray. And God is not so unkind as to call us to pray without showing us the way to do it. In the next chapter, we will discover a simple way that Jesus taught in order to pray successfully.

---

[9]   Elevation Worship, "Rattle", © 2020, from the album *Graves Into Gardens*.

chapter two

A PATTERN FOR PRAYER

It's all too easy to lose our belief in the power of prayer. We address and stamp a package and send it on its way, confident that it will reach its destination. Yet we may doubt that our prayers are heard by a loving Father in heaven. Jesus addressed this uncertainty when he said to the crowds, "So if you sinful people know how to give good gifts to your children, how much more will your heavenly Father give good gifts to those who ask him." [1]

Now God is not some spiritual Father Christmas, who answers our every whim and want. Rather, as Father God, he wants to teach us to pray in line with his will. Then his answers will fill us with awe at his goodness, and help change the world around us. He desires us to become great in prayer. Great prayers, however, are made not born.

---

[1]   Matthew 7:11

We all have to start somewhere. Our praying doesn't have to be perfect. Listen to these genuine prayers from children:

David, aged seven: "Dear God: I need a raise in my allowance. Could you have one of your angels tell my father? Thank you."

Debbie, aged seven: "Dear God: Please send a new baby for Mummy. The new baby you sent last week cries too much."

Angela, aged eight: "Dear God: This is my prayer. Could you please give my brother some brains? So far he doesn't have any."

We may chuckle, but these simple prayers come straight from the heart. Childlike faith and simplicity are the keys to successful prayer, not eloquence. Today's greatest prayer warriors were once babies in the things of the Holy Spirit. The key is to start. Thankfully, Jesus revealed how to do this.

Jesus' Pattern for Prayer

One day, as Jesus spent time in prayer, his disciples listened to him. What they heard so impacted them that they exclaimed, "Lord teach us to pray!" His answer to them has become one of the most beloved prayers in Christianity:

When you pray, say:

Our Father in heaven, hallowed be your name.
Your kingdom come, your will be done on earth
as it is in heaven.
Give us day by day our daily bread.

And forgive us our sins, for we also forgive
everyone who is indebted to us.
And do not lead us into temptation, but deliver
us from the evil one. [2]

Throughout history, millions of Christians have recited
this, the Lord's Prayer, from memory. And while that can be
meaningful, Jesus was actually teaching a pattern to follow,
not a prayer to recite. If we understand this pattern, it will free
us to pray in a way that the Father will hear and answer. It will
also help us to pray the complete will of God into being, not
merely part of it. Two distinct parts make up the prayer, and
we will look at the second part first. There are three important
areas covered in this latter part of the prayer.

Give Us Our Daily Bread.

Here Jesus invites us to pray for the material things we need
for life: finance, work, health, housing, transport, relationships,
guidance, and so on. This is asking for provision. A kind heavenly
Father wants to meet all our legitimate needs for living. We are
to simply ask and thank him for the answer.

A few years ago, when Greta and I ministered overseas for
three months, my six-year-old iPad kept freezing. One day in
a large church, it froze in the middle of my sermon. So I had
to buy a new iPad from an Apple store. The $1150 price tag
was a stretch for our ministry funds at the time, so we asked
our Father to supply the finance, as it was a genuine need.

---

[2]   Luke 11:2-4 (NKJV)

The next day $1000 appeared in our account from a family in our home church back in New Zealand. When I thanked them, I mentioned the need that their gift had met. After they discovered we had paid $1150, they generously gifted another $150 to make up the full amount. It turned out that they were facing a large financial need of their own and had decided to sow into our ministry.

Forgive Us Our Sins as We Forgive Others.

Here we are told to ask the Lord to forgive our sins, help us forgive others, and not hold offence towards them. This is asking for **purity**. Forgiveness is a big issue to God. So big, that his readiness to forgive us of our wrongdoings depends on our willingness to forgive others. "So if you are presenting a sacrifice at the altar in the Temple and you suddenly remember that someone has something against you," instructs Jesus, "leave your sacrifice there at the altar. Go and be reconciled to that person. Then come and offer your sacrifice to God." [3]

In today's context this means that, if we are worshipping God in song, prayer, or any other way and remember we have offended someone, we are to put that right, otherwise our worship is unacceptable to God. Equally, if we worship or pray and someone has offended us, we are to forgive them. Unforgiveness doesn't imprison the offender; it imprisons the offended. When we forgive, it frees us, and frees the Lord to work justice on our behalf.

---

[3]   Matthew 5:23-24

Some years ago, Greta and I conducted a seminar in an Australian city. We taught on how to pray for the sick and then demonstrated how to do it. Through a word of knowledge that someone had lower back pain, a sixty-five-year-old woman responded. She told us that she had suffered pain persistently since the age of five. After we asked what had happened at that time, she explained that as she held her newly born sister, she slipped off the chair she was sitting on, and the baby rolled onto the floor. Though her little sister was thankfully unharmed, she injured her back. Her mother scolded her severely, and the little girl felt offended and hurt that her mum seemed to have no regard for her. As she related the story with fresh tears, we suggested that it was time to forgive her mother, and lift the offence toward her.

We led her in a prayer of forgiveness, then prayed for her back, commanding it to be healed in Jesus' name. Testing her back by bending over, she exclaimed, "The pain is nearly all gone!" After we ministered to her again, she said that there was zero pain. Unforgiveness had held her captive for six decades and prevented her from being healed.

Don't Let Us Be Led into Temptation but Deliver Us from The Evil One.

Here we ask that the Lord will keep us from enticing temptation, and deliver us from Satan's cunning schemes and attacks against us and our family. This is asking for **protection**. We pray, not out of fear, but out of wisdom, to pre-empt any harm that may come to us.

It's a wise thing to pray for God's protection over our health, relationships, finances, children, employment and so on.

"If you make the Lord your refuge, if you make the Most High your shelter," writes the psalmist, "no evil will conquer you; no plague will come near your home. For he will order his angels to protect you wherever you go." [4] The whole angelic realm stands ready to protect those who honour and revere God and stay close to him. This does not mean that we won't face trials and difficulties. Some trials God protects us *from*, others he protects us *in* by sending an angelic squad to escort us through them.

As an illustration, some early North American Indian tribes had a unique practice of graduating young braves to become full warriors in the tribe. On the eve of a boy's thirteenth birthday, after having learned hunting, scouting, and fishing skills, the tribe gave him one final test. He was placed in a dense forest to spend the entire night alone. Until then, he had never been away from the security of the family and the tribe. But on this night, he was blindfolded and taken several miles away.

When he took off the blindfold, he was alone in the middle of thick woods and he was terrified! Strange noises pierced the darkness, making him tremble with fear. After what seemed like an eternity, dawn broke and the first rays of sunlight entered the interior of the forest. Looking around, the boy saw flowers, trees, and the outline of the path. Then, to his astonishment, he beheld the figure of a man standing nearby, armed with a bow and arrow.

---

[4]   Psalm 91:9-11

It was his father. He had been there all night long watching over his son.[5]

And God our Father, with his angels, watches over us.

Summary

The second half of the Lord's Prayer is to do with God granting us provision, purity, and protection. *The second half is all about us.* Because we are God's children through faith in Jesus our saviour, it is completely natural to ask the Father to meet all our needs in life. He delights to do so. And it is good to also pray these things for others whom God brings to mind.

There is a problem, however, in much of the global Church,[6] at least in the West. Too many Christians have camped in the second half of the Lord's Prayer with their prayer lives reduced to asking only for their needs to be met. And as valid as that is, seldom do they venture into the first part. We must realise that Jesus put the first part at the beginning because it is the most important.

In the next chapter, we will discover what the first part is and why it must be a priority.

---

[5] Adapted from www.sermonillustrations.com/a-z/p/protection.htm, accessed 24/06/2021

[6] The use of the capitalised Church throughout this book indicates the worldwide church, as opposed to a single local church.

chapter three

THE PRIORITY FOR PRAYER

In the previous chapter, we discovered that the Lord's Prayer is not merely a prayer to recite, but rather a pattern to follow. The second half of the prayer invites us to ask our heavenly Father for **provision, purity, and protection.** Yet much of the Church has camped in this second half. The Holy Spirit is calling us to make the first part of the Lord's Prayer a priority. While we will continue to ask that God meet our needs, our focus will increasingly shift to the first part. Two important areas are covered in this part of the prayer.

Our Father, Hallowed Be Your Name.

The word *hallowed* means holy, consecrated, sacred, or honoured. To hallow the Father is to praise him, thank him, and pray that his name and the name of Jesus would be esteemed and adored throughout the whole world. This is **worship.**

What a privilege to call Almighty God our Father.[1]

This opening line of the Lord's Prayer shows that prayer is not some obligatory duty or lifeless mechanism to get answers from heaven; rather it is first and foremost a relationship with God. Great praying flows out of great intimacy, for in that place of closeness, we hear Father's heartbeat for our lives and a lost world. As a result, we are better able to pray in his will. "Take delight in the Lord," advised King David, "and he will give you the desires of your heart." [2] In this aspect of prayer, we delight in, and worship, our God. And that can be vocal or in silence; with music or without music. It's enjoying his presence.

During the exodus of Israel from Egypt to the promised land of Canaan, the Israelites angered God. On hearing God say that he would consequently no longer go with the nation, Moses pled with God for his presence to remain with them:

> If your Presence does not go with us, do not send us up from here. How will anyone know that you are pleased with me and with your people unless you go with us? What else will distinguish me and your people from all the other people on the face of the earth? [3]

---

[1] This is made possible through faith in Jesus. John 1:12 states, "But to all who believed him (Jesus) and accepted him (as Messiah and Saviour), he gave the right to become children of God."

[2] Psalm 37:4 (NIV)

[3] Exodus 33:15-16 (NIV)

Astonishingly, God changed his mind and granted Moses' request. "I will indeed do what you have asked," replied the Lord, "for you have found favour with me, and you are my friend." [4] How did Moses become God's friend and find such incredible favour? The earlier part of the chapter reveals the reason: "Now Moses used to take a tent and pitch it outside the camp some distance away, calling it the Tent of Meeting. Anyone inquiring of the Lord would go to the tent of meeting outside the camp." [5]

Moses visited the tent frequently. "Inside the Tent of Meeting, the Lord would speak to Moses face to face, as one speaks to a friend." [6] Through worship and spending time in God's presence, Moses built a friendship with the Lord. This allowed him to ask for extraordinary things and see them granted.

Could it be that Jesus had this incident in mind when he instructed us to start with worship when praying? He, like Moses, embodied a life lived in intimacy with his Father. This inspired great prayers,[7] and great prayers lead to great answers. Amazingly, Moses didn't stop at asking for God's presence – he then asked to see God's glory. "Then Moses had one more request," the Bible records. "Please let me see your glorious presence." [8] And the Lord granted it.[9]

Today, our Father invites us into the same tent of meeting – not a canvas one, but a spiritual one. It is a place where we worship him and his son Jesus, where we discover that we are

---

[4]   Exodus 33:17 (NLT 1996 version)
[5]   Exodus 33:7 (NIV)
[6]   Exodus 33:11
[7]   See John 17 for example where Jesus prays for unity among his followers.
[8]   Exodus 33:18 (NLT 1996 version)
[9]   See Exodus 33:19-23

not only believers, but sons and daughters of God, and friends with him. A darkened world is yet to see the transforming glory that would result from the bold prayers of those that have found favour with God. *Our Father, hallowed be your name* is much more than a nice poetic saying – it is the entrance into a life of effective prayer that can change us and the world around us.

Let Your Kingdom Come, Your Will Be Done On Earth.

"Let your kingdom come" and "let your will be done" are the same thing.[10] The coming of God's kingdom equals God's will being established on earth. Where people submit to God's will, the kingdom rules over them. Conflict results, however, because sinful people and satanic powers will resist that rule. To pray that God's kingdom comes to earth is actually asking for an invasion of heaven and is therefore an act of **war**.

Many people think that to submit to God's will is the worst thing that can happen to them. The opposite is true. "For the kingdom of God is not a matter of eating and drinking," explained the apostle Paul, "but of righteousness, peace and joy in the Holy Spirit." [11] Paul also stated that, "The kingdom of God is not a matter of talk but of power." [12] If adhered to, this incredibly good news would lead to paradise on earth.

---

[10] Jewish poets, psalmists and orators were familiar with the technique of parallelism, where a second statement repeats the meaning of the first by simply changing the words.
[11] Romans 14:17 (NIV)
[12] 1 Corinthians 4:20 (NIV)

And yet the Bible reveals that, "Satan, who is the god of this world, has blinded the minds of those who don't believe. They are unable to see the glorious light of the Good News." [13] Though sin and Satan were both defeated by Christ, multitudes resist God's will in their lives because of deception. In fact, they may actively fight for the opposite, thinking that they are actually doing good.

By his ministry, death, and resurrection, Jesus initiated the coming of the kingdom to earth. We glimpse it in the gospels as we see Jesus heal the sick, break demonic oppression, and reveal God's truth that transforms lives. Before he returned to heaven, Jesus commanded his followers to spread the kingdom of heaven on earth through prayer, and by proclaiming it through words of truth, works of love, and supernatural signs. Every act of healing, deliverance, reconciliation, and kindness now points to the day when Christ returns and there will be no sickness, violence, death, racism, prejudice, suffering, war, oppression, or poverty.

At the beginning of his ministry, Jesus announced, "Repent, for the kingdom of heaven has come near."[14] His mission was to bring God's kingdom to earth. When we pray that his kingdom would come to our lives, family, nation, and nations, we are helping fulfil that mission. The following story reflects how this can happen practically.

---

[13]   2 Corinthians 4:4a (throughout this book, the letter 'a' denotes the first part of the verse)
[14]   Matthew 4:17 (NIV)

A Business Reflects God's Kingdom

Some years ago, my accountant told me the following story. The owner of a photocopying business discussed with a marketplace chaplain how the shop might fulfil Jesus' command to make his kingdom known, and for it to become missional in some way. Realising that people have to wait some time for their jobs to be completed, they came up with a strategy: make waiting a pleasure.

Setting up a comfortable lounge area, the owner made free coffee available, and each day posted on a large notice board secular or Biblical sayings – captivating thoughts to contemplate while waiting. Also, a small sign announced that if anyone had a need, the staff would love to pray for it until it was resolved.

As the prayer requests started to roll in, they grew in number to the point that, for two hours a week, the owner employed a woman with an intercessory heart to handle the prayer load. In this creative way, the business fulfilled Jesus' command to pray that God's kingdom would come to earth.

The Partial and the Full Kingdom

One day, Jesus will return and fully establish his kingdom rule on earth, locking Satan and his hordes in hell, and removing all unrighteous people from earth. Here is a sample of what it will be like: "The Lord will mediate between nations and will settle international disputes. They will hammer their swords into plowshares and their spears into pruning hooks.

Nation will no longer fight against nation, nor train for war anymore." [15] Imagine the vast financial resources that could be diverted to housing and agriculture through no longer having to produce armaments.

So the kingdom is here on earth now, albeit partially. Until Jesus returns, the Church is to engage in prayer and mission that will see the kingdom of God spread to more and more people. When we ask for the salvation of loved ones, our world to be transformed, spiritual awakening to come, governments to be righteous, and spiritual powers of darkness to fall, our praying assumes the correct priority. Our destination might be heaven, but our destiny is to bring heaven to our world. Or as American pastor Bill Johnson puts it, "God's job is to get me to heaven; my job is to bring heaven to earth through my prayers and obedience."

In summary, the first part of the Lord's Prayer teaches that worship of the Father and asking that his kingdom come to earth are to be a priority. This is why the Holy Spirit is shifting our focus from the second part of the prayer to the first. The second part is all about us; the first part is all about him. In fact, Jesus promised, "Seek the Kingdom of God above all else, and live righteously, and he will give you everything you need." [16] If we pray for God's concerns, he will generously answer prayers for our concerns.

---

[15]   Isaiah 2:4 (NIV)
[16]   Matthew 6:33

The Challenge

I love spontaneous prayer. The Christian believer can pray anytime and anywhere: while driving, gardening, working, playing, facing a crisis and so on. Such prayers are usually short, urgent, or simply chatting with the Lord. In 445BC, the Jewish captive Nehemiah was cupbearer to King Xerxes of Persia. The recent news that his beloved Jerusalem was in a state of ruin, and that the Jewish returnees were in distress, saddened him.

Normally, exhibiting sorrow in the king's presence was a capital offence for a cupbearer. Amazingly, rather than have him executed, Xerxes asked why he was sad. The Bible records Nehemiah's response: "With a prayer to the God of heaven, I replied, 'If it please the king, and if you are pleased with me, your servant, send me to Judah to rebuild the city where my ancestors are buried.' " [17] Xerxes agreed and Jerusalem was rebuilt. Nehemiah's spontaneous prayer was heard by God.

There is another type of prayer, however, that is more planned, more deliberate. Jesus described it when he said, "But when you pray, go away by yourself, shut the door behind you, and pray to your Father in private. Then your Father, who sees everything, will reward you." [18] This is *focused* prayer.

Focused prayer is prayer that shuts out the distractions of the world around us. A bedroom, lounge, forest path, strip of beach, neighbourhood footpath, or hilltop – all may become places where we 'shut the door' to be alone with God and pray

---

[17] Nehemiah 2:4b-5 (throughout this book, the letter 'b' denotes the second part of the verse)
[18] Matthew 6:6

according to the pattern of the Lord's prayer.

Here is the challenge – can you give the Lord fifteen minutes or half an hour a day, to invest time in prayer? "The secret of praying," declared Leonard Ravenhill, "is to pray in secret." Some of you may already be achieving this. Then why not go beyond where you are, and ask the Lord to increase your capacity?

Others of you may have almost no focused prayer time at all. Then how about starting with a few minutes each day, and allow the Holy Spirit to build spiritual muscle in you? Pray through the Lord's prayer, section by section, as Jesus taught us.

Start with worship. Thank and praise your Father and Saviour. Open a psalm of praise and pray it back to him. Or listen to some worship music and sing along, or sit in silence, adoring him. That will fill at least five minutes. Then pray that his kingdom comes – pray for the lost people in your life to be saved, for spiritual awakening, for solutions to societal problems, and other areas that the Holy Spirit may show you.

After that, pray for your own needs, for forgiveness, and for protection. Before you know it, fifteen minutes, half an hour or even an hour will have gone by. Don't make it complicated – it's like talking to a friend. And the Holy Spirit will help you. Sometimes the Spirit may stop you at worship and the whole time is spent there. Or it may be the issues of the kingdom, or family needs. Let him set the pace.

In setting a time period to pray, realise that there is a difference between a goal and a law. A law makes you feel guilty if you don't accomplish the time each day. A goal is an aim.

If you miss a day or two, you attempt it again. A law enslaves; a goal inspires.

Now, some of you may be seasoned pray-ers, and you enjoy a more prophetic style of praying,[19] as the Holy Spirit reveals areas to focus on, and how to pray for them. Just make sure, that over time, you cover all the topics contained in the Lord's prayer.

Diligence in Prayer is Vital

"Without prayer," writes Justin Welby,[20] "there will be no renewal of the church and without renewal of the church, there is very little hope for the world." Revivalist John Wesley,[21] founder of the Methodist movement, went further when he said, "God does nothing but in answer to prayer." That is a strong statement, but one which is true. Nothing of real worth is accomplished without prayer. The Lord is sovereign and is able to do things at his initiative, but appears to mainly limit his activity to the prayers of his Church.

That is both alarming and exciting. If we neglect prayer, it will limit what God does in our lives and world. If we are diligent in prayer, he "is able, through his mighty power at work within us, to accomplish infinitely more than we might ask or think."[22] Never underestimate the power of a simple, faith-filled prayer. In these troubled times, prayer that follows the pattern Jesus taught us, will make us victors and not victims.

---

[19] We will discuss prophetic prayer in chapter seven.
[20] Justin Welby, Anglican Archbishop of Canterbury, 1956 -
[21] John Wesley, 1703-1791
[22] Ephesians 3:20

The apostle Peter spoke to every generation when he said, "Since we are approaching the end of all things, be intentional, purposeful, and self-controlled so that you can be given to prayer." [23] If we do, we will see heaven open over our lives and the world around us, and we will be fully awake when Christ returns.

In the next chapter, we will discover the type of prayer that opens heaven.

---

[23]   1 Peter 4:7 (TPT)

chapter four

PRAYER THAT OPENS HEAVEN

Nestled in one of the many valleys common to Wales was a small village of around two hundred residents. A Baptist chapel stood prominently within the settlement, and attracted some twenty members most Sundays. The rest of the community showed little interest in spiritual matters. One Saturday evening, something miraculous occurred. During the night, the Holy Spirit overshadowed the settlement, and convicted everyone of their need to get right with God. The next morning, the entire population made its way to the chapel to seek salvation.

A retired Baptist minister relayed this incident to Greta and me, when we stayed with him and his wife while ministering in Swansea some years ago. He explained that when in theological college in the early 1950's, one of his lecturers had been the pastor of that village chapel, and gave an eye witness account to the students of what had happened.

The visitation occurred during the Welsh Revival of 1904-1905, an outpouring of God's Spirit that came in answer to the desperate prayers of young Evan Roberts[1] and a band of youthful followers. Within six months, one hundred thousand people gave their lives to Christ, and whole communities were transformed, the village above being one of them. That village, and most of Wales, had experienced an open heaven.

Heaven Can Open

Heaven can open. The book of Genesis records one of the earliest mentions of heaven in the Bible. Having left his home in Canaan due to conflict with his brother Esau, the patriarch Jacob travelled eastwards to Mesopotamia to seek refuge with his relatives. On the way, he stopped the night at Bethel to rest. "As he slept," the Bible records, "he dreamed of a stairway that reached from earth to heaven. And he saw the angels of God going up and down on it." [2] Astounded, Jacob exclaimed, "What an awesome place this is! It is none other than the house of God, the very gateway to heaven!" [3]

The words *stairway* and *gateway* suggest that heaven interacts with earth under certain circumstances. Jesus stated to his first disciples that heaven could be opened. Echoing Jacob's words, Jesus said, "I tell you the truth you will all see heaven open and the angels of God going up and down on the Son of Man." [4] His entire ministry was an interaction of heaven with earth.

---

[1]   Evan Roberts, 1878-1951
[2]   Genesis 28:12
[3]   Genesis 28:17
[4]   John 1:51

When heaven opens over a church, town, city, or nation, people are easily saved, healed, and delivered from satanic oppression, as seen in Jesus' ministry.

So how do we obtain an open heaven? In the same way that Jesus did. "When all the people were being baptized," records the Bible, "Jesus was baptized too. *And as he was praying, heaven was opened* and the Holy Spirit descended on him." [5] Prayer is the key to an open heaven. When heaven opens, the Holy Spirit comes upon people, and a gateway is opened for the angelic realm to be very active. Now, it's crucial to know that there are different types of prayer, and they fall into three broad categories. Of these three kinds, there is one that especially opens heaven.

Petition

First, there is *petition*. This is simply asking that our needs be met. As we have seen, this type of prayer is mentioned in the second half of the Lord's Prayer where we are encouraged to ask for provision, purity, and protection. Petition encompasses simple requests, which usually do not need to be endlessly repeated. "When you pray," instructed Jesus, "don't babble on and on as the Gentiles do. They think their prayers are answered merely by repeating their words again and again. Don't be like them, for your Father knows exactly what you need even before you ask him!" [6]

---

[5]   Luke 3:21-22a (NIV), emphasis mine.
[6]   Matthew 6:7-8

Occasionally, when there is human or spiritual opposition to provision, we may need to keep praying until the answer comes. Mostly, however, we simply need to ask, and then believe that it will happen. "Therefore I tell you," promised Jesus, "whatever you ask for in prayer, believe that you have received it, and it will be yours." [7]

When my first wife Jane and I, with our three young sons, moved to Auckland many years ago, we looked for a suitable house to buy. Because Jane used a wheelchair, we hoped to find a one level home, but in the hilly suburbs of the North Shore where we wanted to live, they were rare. So we had a friend draw up plans for a purpose built house that would suit our needs. Then we looked for a section of land to build on.

One day, we discovered a sizeable cluster of sections in the leafy suburb of Forrest Hill. Close to excellent schools and with good motorway access, it would be an ideal location for us. Having owned the land for years, a developer had recently begun to build dwellings on it. We approached a real estate agent, who told us that the owner would not sell us a plot, as he wanted to build on them all.

Because we felt so drawn to the area, we went and stood on a section that we considered suitable, and prayed that the Lord would change the mind of the developer. Next, we approached his manager. The conversation went something like this:

"Would you sell us a section, so that we can build a home suitable for our unique needs?"

---

[7]   Mark 11:24 (NIV)

"We can't sell you a section, but we can build you a house and sell the package to you."

"We won't be able to afford it if you build it. Our own builders can do it far more affordably. And we have a construction plan."

During the conversation we silently petitioned the Lord for favour. Finally, the manager said to us, "Let me talk to my boss. Come back and see me in two weeks." Over that time, we kept thanking the Lord for the land and often would drive into the sub-development, declaring that one day we would live in it.

A fortnight later, we saw the manager again, who told us that the developer had kindly agreed to our request. The only stipulation was that we would build to a quality comparable to the other houses in the development, which we happily agreed to. When the real estate agent heard our news, she couldn't believe it, saying, "He never sells sections to the public, and he never changes his mind!" Five months later, we moved into our new home.

Petition certainly opens heaven in the sense of God blessing us with answers to our genuine needs. But it is not the type of prayer that opens heaven in the way that transformed the Welsh village mentioned at the beginning of this chapter.

Devotion

The second type of prayer is devotion. Devotional prayer is expressing love for God. As mentioned in the last chapter, it may involve worship, praying through psalms of praise, or sitting quietly in his presence. It is the "hallowed be your name" part of the Lord's prayer. It is time alone with the God who loves us. "Without solitude," said Catholic theologian Henri Nouwen,[8] "it is virtually impossible to live a spiritual life." Jesus knew and practised this. "Very early in the morning, while it was still dark," records the gospel of Mark, "Jesus got up, left the house and went off to a solitary place, where he prayed." [9]

I once heard the following story about missionary statesman Walter Beuttler.[10] Having travelled the world to minister God's word for many years, he finally retired. Admitting to himself that he had often sought God for a sermon, or power in his ministry, he declared that from that point on, he would seek the Lord simply to be near to him. So began a daily habit of rising early to sit in a comfortable chair in his office, with Bible open. There he would meditate on scripture, and converse with the Lord, or simply sit, lost in admiration for his saviour.

One morning, after about six weeks of this daily devotion, Beuttler heard footsteps in the hallway outside his office. *My wife is not normally up at this hour* he thought to himself. The footsteps finally stopped outside the office door, and the door swung open. Because his chair had its back to the entrance, he could not see who had entered the room. At that moment, the room filled with the presence of Jesus and the Holy Spirit opened Beuttler's eyes to see Jesus walk in and stand behind the chair.

After a little time, he felt fine droplets of water falling on him. As he looked up, he saw Jesus weeping over him. When he

---

8   Henri Nouwen, 1932-1996
9   Mark 1:35 (NIV)
10   Walter Beuttler, 1904-1974

asked why the Lord was weeping, Jesus replied, "It is because I so love your fellowship." Walter then positioned a second chair facing his so that the Lord could sit in it.

It seems that God longs for our devotion more than we do. Devotional prayer is a means to intimacy with him. The dictionary defines intimacy as *a close or warm friendship; a belonging together.* And that is what the Father offers us through his son Jesus. May we be like King David who said, "My heart has heard you say, 'Come and talk with me.' And my heart responds, 'Lord, I am coming.' " [11]

Devotional praying may open heaven over us personally, so that we can enjoy God's presence. Nevertheless, it is still not the type of prayer that will open heaven over a town or nation. It is the third type of prayer that enables that.

Intercession

Intercession is persistent prayer that sees salvation, breakthroughs, miracles, victory, revivals, and so on. It is the "let your kingdom come, and your will be done on earth" part of the Lord's prayer. Intercessory prayer is the type of prayer that opens heaven and changes our world.

A passivity often envelops many believers' prayer lives, and a mystique about intercession keeps them from this powerful type of prayer. When our praying starts to change the world, the devil becomes scared.

[11]   Psalm 27:8

Because this kind of prayer is a key to the supernatural, evil spirits work hard to keep us passive, busy, or intimidated. Many believers never move beyond petition and devotion because intercession scares or confuses them.

In fact, many have swallowed the lie that intercession is a special gift for some, but not them. They hear stories of 'intercessors' being woken in the night to pray for others, or who pray with fiery passion, or who have amazing revelation that helps them pray. Indeed, there are people like this in churches. They are ones who usually have a prophetic grace gift that enables them to see into the spiritual realm, and pray accordingly. And we thank God for those so gifted.

But, while not all believers have a *gift* of prophetic intercession, all have the *role* of intercession, just as not all have the gift of evangelism, but all have the role of being a witness for Christ. There is a difference between a gift and a role. I don't have the gift of putting out the rubbish bin for collection each week. It's a role, and if I don't do it, the house will smell. The Lord's Prayer reveals a pattern of praying that is for *all* believers in Jesus, not only a few. Intercession is part of that pattern, and Jesus puts it right behind worship in its priority. Hence, we are all called to intercede.

For many years, Suzette Hattingh[12] was the prayer director for evangelist Reinhard Bonnke's[13] crusades in Africa. Years ago, she visited our church in Auckland, and said emphatically:

---

[12]   Suzette Hattingh, *Voice in the City* ministries, Germany.
[13]   Reinhard Bonnke, 1940 - 2019

Who is called to intercession? All! Intercession is not an office – it is a supportive ministry and belongs to the entire body of Christ. There are only five Biblical offices: apostle, prophet, evangelist, pastor and teacher. You need a call to be a prophet or pastor, but you do not need a call to be an intercessor.

The Holy Spirit is the greatest intercessor and he has been poured out on all of us. Intercession belongs to the entire body of Christ and the sooner the entire body gets it, the sooner we will see oppressed people set free. Intercession is not for a secluded group. The more you pray, the more God will show you his heart. [14]

Persistence is the Hallmark of Intercession

Intercession requires persistence. As we have seen already, Jesus warned us not to be repetitive when petitioning God about our basic needs.[15] And yet, a little later in the same sermon, he says, "Keep on asking, and you will receive what you ask for. Keep on seeking, and you will find. Keep on knocking, and the door will be opened to you. For everyone who asks, receives. Everyone who seeks, finds. And to everyone who knocks, the door will be opened." [16] Here he is describing intercession, and if we confuse the simple prayer of petition with the persistence needed for intercession, we will become discouraged. We will pray a few times for a breakthrough and then give up.

---

[14] Quoted from *The Power of Intercession* seminar, 12 September, 1989.
[15] See Matthew 6:7-8
[16] Matthew 7:7-8

In teaching his disciples further about intercession, Jesus used this story:

> Suppose you went to a friend's house at midnight, wanting to borrow three loaves of bread. You say to him, 'A friend of mine has just arrived for a visit, and I have nothing for him to eat.' And suppose he calls out from his bedroom, 'Don't bother me. The door is locked for the night, and my family and I are all in bed. I can't help you.' But I tell you this – though he won't do it for friendship's sake, if you keep knocking long enough, he will get up and give you whatever you need because of your shameless persistence. [17]

The message here is not that God is reluctant to answer prayer; rather it is that we should have bold persistence in prayer. It is the midnight hour of history. Multitudes are starving for the bread of God's word that could save them and bring them hope. When an emboldened Church persistently knocks on heaven's door, the bread will be released to them.

In the next chapter, we will lift the veil of mystery around intercession, and look at what it really is.

---

[17]   Luke 11:5-8

chapter five

INTERCESSION – EVERYONE CAN DO IT

In the preceding chapter we saw that intercession is the type of prayer that causes heaven to break in upon earth. We also discovered that Jesus instructed every believer to intercede because it is part of the Lord's Prayer. So what is intercessory prayer really like? If we understand it, we will be able to do it.

Intercession Is Like Standing in The Gap

First, intercession is like standing in the gap. The word *intercession* is from the Latin *inter* (meaning between) and *cedere* (meaning to go). Thus, the word simply means *to go between* or *stand in the gap*.

During the exodus of Israel from Egypt to Canaan, Moses spent forty days on Mount Sinai where God gave him the Ten Commandments and other laws to govern Israel.

Without their leader for almost six weeks, the Israelites grew tired of waiting. Perhaps thinking that God had taken him to heaven like Enoch,[1] they asked Moses' brother Aaron to make them a golden calf through which they could worship God. No doubt they had seen the Egyptians worshipping their bull god in Egypt. In an act of betrayal of the gracious God who had delivered them from slavery, they chose to adopt a similar idol. Idolatry is highly infectious and is such a serious sin in God's eyes that he told Moses that he would have to destroy the whole nation.

"But Moses, his chosen one," records the Bible, "*stepped between the Lord and the people. He begged him to turn from his anger and not destroy them.*" [2] This is a perfect picture of true intercession. Furthermore, the Bible records Moses' prayer of intercession:

> O Lord! Why are you so angry with your own people whom you brought from the land of Egypt with such great power and such a strong hand? Why let the Egyptians say, 'Their God rescued them with the evil intention of slaughtering them in the mountains and wiping them from the face of the earth'? Turn away from your fierce anger. Change your mind about this terrible disaster you have threatened against your people!

---

[1]   According to the apocryphal Book of Enoch, Enoch spent much time being translated to heaven in visions. Finally, God took him there permanently. See Genesis 5:22-24 and Hebrews 11:5.

[2]   Psalm 106:23, emphasis mine.

Remember your servants Abraham, Isaac, and Jacob. You bound yourself with an oath to them, saying, 'I will make your descendants as numerous as the stars of heaven. And I will give them all of this land that I have promised to your descendants, and they will possess it forever.' [3]

Because he appealed so strongly to God concerning the Lord's reputation and the promises made to Israel's patriarchs, Moses saved the nation from annihilation: "So the Lord changed his mind about the terrible disaster he had threatened to bring on his people." [4]

Incense Saves the Day

On another occasion, a plague broke out amongst the Israelites, and thousands began to die. Aaron, acting on Moses' instructions, took an incense burner and stood in the gap. "The plague had already started among the people," records the Bible, "but Aaron offered the incense and made atonement for them. *He stood between the living and the dead*, and the plague stopped." [5] Interestingly, the Bible reveals that incense symbolises prayer. In a vision of heaven, the apostle John records, "The twenty-four elders fell down before the Lamb. Each one had a harp, and they held gold bowls filled with incense, which are the prayers of God's people." [6]

---

[3]   Exodus 32:11-13
[4]   Exodus 32:14
[5]   Numbers 16: 47, 48 (NIV), emphasis mine.
[6]   Revelation 5:8

Aaron standing with an incense burner between the people and the plague is thus a beautiful picture of believers who burn with a spirit of prayer, interceding for a lost world plagued by the destructive consequences of sin. They stand in the gap between heaven and hell, health and sickness, life and death, salvation and damnation, and pray for loved ones, cities, nations, and people groups. They appeal to heaven for breakthrough, and stand against the oppression that satanic forces bring.

God laments when he can find no intercessors. "I looked for someone among them," he said to Ezekiel, "who would build up the wall and stand before me in the gap on behalf of the land so I would not have to destroy it, but I found no one." [7] This is why, in the New Covenant, he calls all believers to intercede. There are serious consequences for a nation if we don't. If we obey Jesus' teaching about the Lord's Prayer, there should never again be a vacant gap. In the ultimate act of intercession, God allowed Jesus to bridge the gap between a lost world and himself, through the cross. And he calls us to do the same through prayer. In 1989, a Brazilian woman did exactly that.

A Miracle in Brazil

At that time, Elizabeth Cornelio became concerned about her city, Goiania, then with a population of 1.2 million people, and a major centre of Spiritism. With the city having many other serious problems, she began to meet for prayer with four women from other churches. Four years later, she invited Christians from all over the city to unite and pray.

---

[7]   Ezekiel 22:30 (NIV)

Eight hundred and fifty people joined together for the first prayer meeting. The movement grew rapidly until nearly 200 thousand women prayed every morning for the city.

Elizabeth's daily radio broadcast brought targeted reports on criminal trends to the intercessors. Together they prayed, and a city was changed. After prayer, women went out in the marketplace to pray, simply blessing those around them. When the broadcast was cancelled for three months, the crime rate rose forty percent. The mayor and chief of police pleaded for the programme to be reinstated, and the crime rate receded. It was commonly said that the intercessors were ruling the city, not the mayor!

Mobile prayer teams went door to door. Most weekends around one hundred and fifty people came to Christ, and a new church would begin. As thousands prayed, every church in the city grew and new churches were planted. In seven years, evangelicals in Goiania went from seven percent of the population to forty-five percent. Today the Church in Goiania is known as a place where 'revival is a lifestyle'. [8]

A Korean pastor once said, "In the West you believe in prayer; in Korea we believe in praying." It seems that Brazilians believe that as well. Believing that intercession and other forms of prayer are powerful is of no use, unless we actually pray. But when we do, it gives birth to the impossible.

---

[8]   Adapted from https://renewaljournal.com/2014/04/16/revival-in-brazil-transformationthroughprayer. Accessed 27/7/21

Intercession Is Like Giving Birth

Not only is intercession like standing in the gap, it is also like giving birth. "In the beginning God created the heavens and the earth," records the Bible. "The earth was formless and empty, and darkness covered the deep waters. And the Spirit of God was hovering over the surface of the waters." [9] The Hebrew word for *hovering*, when translated, does not mean inactivity, but rather a pulsating or vibrating, a sweeping back and forth. It implies that the Holy Spirit energetically and eagerly waited for the command from heaven to create or give birth to something.

And when it came, he went to work. "Then God said, 'Let there be light,' and there was light." [10] As various commands came from the Father, through the Son, [11] the Holy Spirit, being the executive member of the Trinity, executed or carried them out. [12] Out of darkness came light, and out of chaos, came order. A whole new world was birthed.

Similarly, when an angel told Mary that she would conceive and give birth to the long awaited Messiah, she asked how that could happen, since she was a virgin. The angel replied, "The Holy Spirit will come upon you, and the power of the Most High will overshadow you. So the baby to be born will be holy, and he will be called the Son of God." [13] Here, the word

---

[9]   Genesis 1:1-2

[10]   Genesis 1:3

[11]   John 1:1-3, speaking of the Son, records, "In the beginning the Word already existed. The Word was with God and the Word was God. He existed in the beginning with God. God created everything through him, and nothing was created except through him."

[12]   See Genesis 1:4-31

[13]   Luke 1:35

overshadow is similar to the word *hovering* in Genesis. Through this overshadowing, Mary miraculously conceived, and nine months later, Jesus was born.

It is like this with intercession. The Holy Spirit hovers over, or overshadows people, businesses, governments, towns, cities, and nations waiting for the Father's command to create life and bring light into darkness. That command is given when we intercede in Jesus' name. Through fellowship with God, a dream, vision, or thought is conceived in us. We then incubate it by interceding in the power of the Holy Spirit until the Father says, "Let there be!" As we keep pushing in prayer, the answer is then birthed, sometimes quickly, other times slowly. This is prayer that births the impossible, opens heaven, and changes our world.

An Experiment

Some years ago, a church in Phoenix, Arizona conducted an experiment. They randomly selected 160 names from the local telephone book and divided the names into two equal groups. For three months, they prayed for one group of eighty homes, but they did not intercede for the other eighty homes.

Afterwards, they called all 160 homes, identified themselves and their church, and asked for permission to stop by and pray for the family and any needs they might have. Of the eighty homes for which they didn't pray, only one invited them to visit. Of the eighty homes for which they had prayed, sixty-nine invited someone to come over.

The Holy Spirit overshadowed all 160 homes,[14] but intercession broke satanic blindness and attracted a command from heaven for the Spirit to bring light to those eighty who were prayed for. And eighty-six percent of them responded. A missionary for seventy years, Dr Wesley Duewel [15] could say with some authority, "Prayer is the final armament! Prayer is the all-inclusive strategy of war. It is a form of spiritual bombing to saturate any area before God's army of witnesses begin their advance. Prayer is the all-conquering, invincible weapon of the army of God."

In summary, we have seen that intercession is like standing in the gap so that God's will would be done on earth as it is in heaven. Intercession is also like giving birth, involving conception, gestation, and labour until the impossible finally arrives. Intercession is prayer that opens heaven, and every believer can know the privilege of co-creating with God as he brings light and order into the darkness and chaos of our world.

In the next chapter we will look at the practicalities of how to intercede.

---

14   In John 16:8, Jesus promised that when the Holy Spirit came, he would convict the world of its sin, and of God's righteousness, and of the coming judgment. The world means all people, everywhere.
15   Wesley Duewel, 1916-2016

chapter six

HOW TO INTERCEDE

In the previous chapter, we discovered what intercession is, and its power to open heaven and bring transformation. In this chapter, we'll look at some of the practicalities of how to do it.

Styles of Intercession

First, there is no one style of intercession that is more powerful than another. How we intercede depends on our personality or the occasion. For example, the Bible records that, "While Jesus was here on earth, he offered prayers and pleadings, with a loud cry and tears, to the one who could rescue him from death. And God heard his prayers because of his deep reverence for God." [1] Jesus prayed loudly, at least on this occasion, and most probably others.

---

[1]   Hebrews 5:7

I have been in prayer meetings with Africans, Asians, and South Americans, and they pray loudly and passionately. Westerners tend on average to be quieter, though that may depend on their denominational background. I am a noisy prayer. Many years ago, when pastoring in New Zealand's capital city Wellington, I had an office in the front of our house where I would pray. One day, as I was interceding, I heard the doorbell ring, and my son Joseph – a pre-schooler at the time – answered the door. A visitor wanted to see me, but Joseph matter-of-factly announced that I was busy shouting at God!

Noise, however, is not a requirement for authentic intercession. Unable to have a baby, Hannah was a grieving woman. Her husband's other wife Peninnah, having borne children, cruelly tormented her year after year. Finally, Hannah grew desperate. The Bible says, "In her deep anguish, Hannah prayed to the Lord, weeping bitterly." [2] She implored God to open her womb, even promising to dedicate her longed-for child back to him. The scriptures then describe the way she prayed: "Hannah was praying in her heart, and her lips were moving but her voice was not heard." [3]

Both Jesus and Hannah interceded with passion and tears. Jesus prayed loudly; Hannah prayed silently. Both styles of intercession were valid, and God answered their prayers. Jesus was delivered from death at the resurrection, and Hannah gave birth to Samuel, who would become one of Israel's greatest prophets. God would also give her other children.

---

[2]   1 Samuel 1:10 (NIV)
[3]   1 Samuel 1:13 (NIV)

Another occasional style of intercession is groaning. "And in a similar way," writes the apostle Paul, "the Holy Spirit takes hold of us in our human frailty to empower us in our weakness. For example, at times we don't even know how to pray, or know the best things to ask for. But the Holy Spirit rises up within us to super-intercede[4] on our behalf, pleading to God with emotional sighs too deep for words." [5] Occasionally, in our Schools of the Supernatural, Greta and I have observed some people doubled over,[6] and groaning with intense passion. Clearly, the Holy Spirit was birthing something wonderful in, or through, them.

So intercession styles can span silence all the way through to loud cries and groanings, and everything in between. Whatever form we may favour, the occasion will sometimes demand a different approach (when in public spaces for example), but when we pray from our hearts, each style is as powerful as the other.

Mix Devotion and Intercession

Second, when praying, mix devotion and intercession, or have separate times of both. British prophet Graham Cooke [7] advises, "Relaxation is for devotion; intensity is for intercession." If all our praying is intense intercession, we will become worn out, and lose the joy of prayer.

---

[4]   The Greek word in the original scripture is *hyperentynchanei* which literally means to make hyper-intercession.
[5]   Romans 8:26 (TPT)
[6]   This is apparently similar to the ancient Middle Eastern birthing position.
[7]   Graham Cooke, *Brilliant Perspectives* ministries, USA.

Conversely, if it's all devotion, we may become too passive. We need a balance of both, as revealed in the first part of the Lord's Prayer.

Jesus loved to visit the home of his friend Lazarus, and his sisters Martha and Mary, in the village of Bethany. It was a place of respite from the demands of ministry for him. One time, Martha busied herself preparing a meal for Jesus and the other guests that were with him. Mary, however, sat at Jesus' feet, listening devotedly to every word he spoke. Irritated, Martha asked Jesus to tell her sister to help her with the meal. Jesus simply replied, "My dear Martha, you are worried and upset over all these details! There is only one thing worth being concerned about. Mary has discovered it, and it will not be taken away from her." [8]

Jesus did not devalue the need for practical service; rather he emphasised the priority of devotion — we are not to sit after serving; rather we are to serve after sitting. Interceding that God's kingdom would come to this broken planet is heady business. If we don't take time to sit at the Lord's feet in simple devotion and worship, we can feel overwhelmed with the task.

Just Do It

Third, just do it! The best way to learn to pray is to pray. The less we pray, the less we will want to pray; the more we pray, the more we will want to pray. Irish hymn writer Joseph Scriven [9] was correct when he penned, "What a friend we have

---

[8]   Luke 10:41-42
[9]   Joseph M. Scriven, 1819-1886

in Jesus, all our sins and griefs to bear; What a privilege to carry everything to God in prayer." [10] Or as French Archbishop Francois Frenelon [11] wrote:

> Tell God all that is in your heart, as one unloads one's heart, its pleasures and its pains, to a dear friend. Tell him your troubles, that he may comfort you; tell him your joys, that he may sober them; tell him your longings that he may purify them; tell him your dislikes that he may help you conquer them; talk to him of your temptations, that he may shield you from them; show him the wounds of your heart, that he may heal them...in other words, tell God everything - both good and bad - with an attitude of openness.

Whether it is devotion, petition, or intercession, talk to God like a friend.

Group Prayer

Fourth, some prayers are only answered when believers pray together. "I also tell you this," promised Jesus, "If two of you agree here on earth concerning anything you ask, my Father in heaven will do it for you." [12] While praying alone is very effective, praying with others of like mind and passion, is even more effective, whether it be in a small group or a large gathering.

---

[10] First verse of *What a Friend We Have in Jesus* © Universal Pictures Music, Jrm Music, Word Music.
[11] Francois Frenelon, 1651-1715
[12] Matthew 18:19

Our home church, Church Unlimited in Auckland, has a one hour, well-attended churchwide prayer meeting from 6pm to 7pm each week. After fifteen minutes of worship, we pray for forty-five minutes using power point slides as prompts for different topics, and we all intercede simultaneously, or sometimes in groups of two or three. It may seem very structured but there is always openness to the leading of the Holy Spirit. This way, the hour goes fast and people appreciate getting home to their families. Too many church prayer meetings drag on and are frankly boring if a few longwinded pray-ers dominate. All manner of prayer is also threaded throughout the life of the church, including half nights of prayer every few months.

Interceding together in unity, especially for city, national, and global issues, definitely causes God to lend his ear to our requests.

More Prayer Is Better Than Less Prayer

Fifth, when we commit to focused prayer, whether devotion, petition, or intercession, Satan will try and condemn us. Suppose you have only been a spontaneous pray-er and now you commit to ten to fifteen minutes of focused prayer a day. Once you begin to achieve that, the enemy will whisper, "How pathetic. What difference does your paltry few minutes of prayer make? You should pray longer." The devil doesn't actually want you to pray longer – he is trying to shame you into giving up.

So you work harder at focused prayer and manage half an hour a day. Feeling encouraged, you then hear the enemy say, "So you think half an hour is good? Didn't Jesus say to his disciples, 'Could you not watch and pray for *an hour?*' " Then if you attain an hour, he will point out someone who prays longer than that. By condemnation and comparison, Satan will try to make you a slave to the clock, suggesting that you are acceptable to God only when you pray for a certain time each day. Very quickly, the joy of prayer will evaporate.

The only way to counter this is to declare that *more prayer is better than less prayer.* Tell the devil, "Be gone Satan! My fifteen minutes of prayer today is better than none before. My half an hour or hour today is better than my fifteen minutes yesterday." Each time he tries to condemn you for whatever length of time you pray, tell him the same thing. He will soon leave you alone and it will free you from slavery to performance and the clock.

Deal with Obstacles

Once we embark on this great adventure of prayer, we will soon encounter many obstacles. At times, for example, prayer may be the last thing we feel like doing. That is our human nature – or weak flesh as Jesus called it – talking. In such times, if we pray regardless of how we feel, the Holy Spirit will empower us in our weakness. Some of my most powerful times of prayer have been when I have felt least like praying. At other times, we may desire to pray, but then find it is difficult to get into the flow of prayer. If we push through this barrier, that same divine empowering will meet us.

As Victorian preacher George Muller[13] warned:

> It is a common temptation of Satan to make us give up the reading of the Word and prayer when our enjoyment is gone; as if it were of no use to read the Scriptures when we do not enjoy them, and as if it were no use to pray when we have no spirit of prayer. The truth is that in order to enjoy the Word, we ought to continue to read it, and the way to obtain a spirit of prayer is to continue praying.

Another obstacle to prayer is distraction. While praying, our mind may wander far and wide, and it is hard to focus. Some of these distractions – especially ones that condemn us or make us fearful – are from the enemy and need to be resisted. Others might be legitimate things we need to attend to and may even be the Lord reminding us to action them. The best way to deal with these is to write them down to attend to later. Once written down, they won't keep plaguing us during our time of prayer.

In this hectic modern world with all its stresses and concerns, busyness is also a common obstacle to prayer. "If you have so much business to attend to that you have no time to pray," said evangelist D. L. Moody,[14] "depend upon it, you have more business on hand than God ever intended you should have." Or as author and theologian C. S. Lewis[15] expressed, "The moment you wake up each morning, all your wishes and hopes for the day rush at you like wild animals. And the first job each morning consists in shoving it all back; in listening to that other

---

[13] George Muller, 1805-1898
[14] D. L. Moody, 1837-1899
[15] C. S. Lewis, 1898-1963

voice, taking that other point of view, letting that other, larger, stronger, quieter life come flowing in."

It seems counter-intuitive, but when we think that we don't have enough time in the day to get everything done, giving time to prayer actually strengthens us for the tasks at hand and makes us more productive. "Using a dull axe requires great strength," advised King Solomon, "so sharpen the blade." [16] When we spend time in prayer and in God's word, he will bless us with wisdom and divine energy to accomplish what is important, and ignore what isn't.

How is Your Path?

The story is told that early African converts to Christianity were earnest and regular in private devotions. Each one reportedly had a separate spot in the bush where he or she would pour out their heart to God. Over time, the paths to these places became well worn. As a result, if one of these believers began to neglect prayer, it was soon plain to the others. They would kindly remind the negligent one, "Friend, the grass grows on your path." [17] The question we must ask ourselves is, "How is our path?" Is it overgrown? Or is it worn bare?

In the next chapter, we will discover an exciting way of praying that the Holy Spirit may lead us into from time to time.

---

[16] Ecclesiastes 10:10
[17] Adapted from *Today in the Word*, June 29, 1992.

chapter seven

PROPHETIC PRAYER

In previous chapters, we have examined the pattern of prayer that Jesus taught in the Lord's Prayer. Following that pattern is an invaluable aid to an effective prayer life. As we mature, however, we may find that occasionally we step into prophetic praying. Before we describe this potent type of prayer, let's first look at what prophecy is.

Prophecy

"People do not live by bread alone," declared Jesus, "but by every word that comes from the mouth of God." [1] While life's material necessities are important, and while God richly supplies us with all things to enjoy,[2] a life focused on material things alone is an empty life. This is why God desires to speak to his people constantly. To truly live, we need to hear God's voice.

---

[1]   Matthew 4:4
[2]   See 1 Timothy 6:17

The principal way that the Lord speaks to us is through the Bible. If we regularly read scripture,[3] we show him that we value his words, and he will be more inclined to speak to us in other ways as well. Prophecy is one of those ways, along with dreams, visions, impressions and so on. All these can bring guidance and inspiration to our lives, but must agree with the Bible.

Simply put, prophecy is speaking a message of encouragement from God.[4] This may include predicting the future (foretelling) or explaining the present (forthtelling). "One who prophesies," instructs the apostle Paul, "is helping others grow in the Lord, encouraging and comforting them." [5] Prophecy is hearing God speak, and then sharing what he says. Some Christians say that God never talks to them. Actually, he is always speaking, but we need to understand how to tune our spiritual ears to his wavelength.

Ways to Hear God's Voice

There are many ways that enable us to hear God's voice, but we can condense them into three main ones. First, there is *seeing*. This is a pictorial way of hearing – God speaks in a mental picture, vision, or dream. At times, what is seen may be symbolic and therefore will need an interpretation. For example, when praying for a young couple once, I saw in my mind a

---

[3]   The dictionary defines scripture to mean: "the sacred writings of Christianity contained in the Bible".

[4]   At times, prophecy may also include correction or direction, but these kinds of prophetic words are best left to those mature in the use of the gift, or prophets. It is not within the scope of this book to discuss prophecy in detail.

[5]   1 Corinthians 14:3

question mark. As I watched, it changed to an exclamation mark. Quickly praying for understanding, I then explained that they had been in a *why?* season, asking why so many painful things had happened to them. This brought them to tears, but they smiled when I said, "But God will change your *why?* season to a *wow!* season."

Second, there is *feeling*. Here a person feels what another person is feeling, or what God is feeling, or feels the atmosphere of the location they are in. When Greta and I visited a certain city in Europe some years ago, I felt a very heavy oppression, and thought that it was just me feeling depressed. As I prayed about it, the Holy Spirit showed me that a spirit of death sat over the city. It turned out that city had one of the highest death and suicide rates of any metropolis in Europe. The Lord revealed this by letting me feel it, so that Greta and I could pray appropriately.

At other times, a person may feel great joy when praying, and that usually indicates that the individual or situation they are interceding for will experience something very good.

Third, there is *hearing*. Here God speaks in words, phrases, or whole sentences. God will speak like we talk and think, so as not to frighten us with an other-worldly voice. Therefore, we may think it is us making it up. In 1995, while living in South Africa, Greta and her first husband Ron prayed about where they should live. The Lord said to them, "Go to New Zealand, I tell you go." With an internationally recognised degree in physiotherapy, Greta had unsolicited job offers from the United States, Canada, and the United Kingdom – all with far better pay rates than New Zealand. But they obeyed God and immigrated to New Zealand, where Ron would pass away eleven years later, and the Lord would lead Greta and me to meet and marry. I am very grateful that they heard God speak to them.

If what we see, feel, or hear is meant to be shared with others, then as we begin to prophesy the little that we have, more will come.

The Link Between Prophecy and Prayer

So how does hearing God's voice apply to prayer? To understand this, we need to look at an important rule of biblical interpretation: the principle of first mention. This states that when a topic is mentioned in the Bible for the very first time, the verse in which it occurs contains the essential truth about that topic. As it happens, the first mention of the word *prophet* in the Bible is found when God warned Abimilech, king of the Philistines, to return Abraham's wife Sarah to him: "Now return the woman to her husband," he said, "and he will pray for you, for he is a prophet. Then you will live." [6] The words *pray*, *prophet*, and *live* are significant. God has designed prophecy to bring life. In addition, prophecy and prayer are closely linked.

First, all prophecy is an invitation to intercession. We need to mix every true prophetic word we receive with faith, and pray until it happens, however long it takes. Second, there will be times in prayer that prophetic revelation may come to enable us to pray more specifically about a matter, or to pray something that we had not thought to. This is called prophetic prayer.

---

[6]   Genesis 20:7a

We are not following a pattern, a prayer list, or our own thoughts. Rather, the Holy Spirit speaks to us, and directs our praying. We may see a picture, feel something, hear thoughts, or have a scripture come to mind. This is a sign that we should begin to pray along the lines of what we are seeing, feeling, or hearing. As we pray, further insight may come.

Examples of Prophetic Prayer

In the days of evil King Ahab of Israel, the prophet Elijah prophesied that there would be drought over the nation for three years. This was a disciplinary action of God due to the nation's worship of the false god Baal. After a contest with the prophets of Baal on Mt Carmel, where Elijah called down fire from heaven, the Israelites bowed in worship to God and forsook their devotion to Baal. Because of this, they fulfilled the conditions for the drought to be broken. Elijah then said to Ahab, "I hear a mighty rainstorm coming!" [7] He did not hear it physically, for the rain hadn't yet started, but heard it in his spirit. As a result, he began to engage in prophetic prayer, asking God to fulfil what he was hearing.

"Elijah climbed to the top of Mount Carmel," records the Bible, "and bowed low to the ground and prayed with his face between his knees." [8] Adopting a birthing position of intercession, Elijah prayed fervently for the rain to come. Every so often, he asked his servant to look out to sea and report if there was any sign of the impending rain. "The servant went and looked, then returned to Elijah and said, 'I didn't see anything.'

---

[7]   1 Kings 18:41
[8]   1 Kings 18:42

Seven times Elijah told him to go and look. Finally, after the seventh time, his servant told him, 'I saw a little cloud about the size of a man's hand rising from the sea.' " [9]

In prophetic prayer it is vital that we persevere, in order that God may fulfil what he reveals to us. If Elijah had given up after the fifth or even sixth time he prayed, the answer would have been aborted. Yet he persisted, and though it began to materialise in a tiny way, the breakthrough came: "Soon the sky was black with clouds. A heavy wind brought a terrific rainstorm." [10]

That's all very well for Elijah, some may think, feeling that they are in no way like him. Yet the Bible declares, "The earnest prayer of a righteous person has great power and produces wonderful results. Elijah was as human as we are, and yet when he prayed that no rain would fall, none fell for three and a half years! Then, when he prayed again, the sky sent down rain and the earth began to yield its crops." [11]

A Current Prophecy About Spiritual Rain

Several years ago, while we were ministering in Australia, Greta was woken in the middle of the night by the thunderous sound of a heavy deluge of rain. She writes, "While listening to the downpour, a prophetic word for the nations came to me, which I wrote down as I heard it. 1 Kings 18:41-45 was a key scripture where Elijah was bent over on top of Mount Carmel

---

[9]   1 Kings 18:43b-44
[10]   1 Kings 18:45
[11]   James 5:16b-18

under a cloudless sky."

Here is some of what God said to her:

Can it be? Go again!

Can it be that a nation be born in a day?

Can it be that a city be fully awakened to me?

Can it be that dead dry bones can live?

Can it be that I pour out my Spirit upon all flesh and manifest signs, wonders and miracles for the display of my splendour?

Go again!

Go again to the mountain of prayer.

Go again to the mountain of my presence.

Cry out to me and I will answer from heaven.

Prophesy, 'Let it rain.'

From the mountain top you will see a cloud the size of a man's fist.

Go again! You will see the cloud approaching.

Go again! You will feel the wind coming stronger.

See if I will not open the floodgates of heaven and rain down my Spirit to bring life to the desert places.

See if I will not blow the wind of my Spirit to breathe life into the dead dry bones that will become a mighty army of the Lord in this nation.

I AM he who can do every *can it be*.

I have decreed *life* over this nation and it shall happen if you *go again*.

Greta continues, "I sensed the Lord say, 'Like Elijah declared under a silent, clear sky, prophesy over the nation: *there is the sound of heavy rain*. Then, like him, pray and keep praying for the outpouring of the Spirit on all the nations.' God will open the floodgates of heavens, if we humble ourselves, turn from our sinful ways, and keep persevering in prayer." [12]

A Prophetic Prayer Strategy for the Muslim World

For more than thirty years, I have prayed for the Islamic world, asking that Muslims may have a revelation of Jesus Christ, and come to know the Father's love for them. Some years ago, while in prayer, the Holy Spirit impressed the word *disillusionment* on my mind. Then he said, "Pray that a great disillusionment will come upon the Islamic world."

---

[12] See 2 Chronicles 7:14 (NIV): "If my people, who are called by my name, will humble themselves and pray and seek my face and turn from their wicked ways, then I will hear from heaven, and I will forgive their sin and will heal their land."

I believe that I heard God's strategy to win millions of Muslims to himself. Ever since, I have prayed that way, and increasingly seen reports of exactly that happening. Disturbed by the senseless slaughter of not only westerners but their own people by Islamic extremists, more and more Muslims are saying, "If this is what our faith is, then we don't want it." While some are becoming secular, others are turning to Christ, especially as the Lord gives them dreams or visions about himself. Many believers around the world continue to intercede for the Muslim world, and God is answering them.

Conclusion

These examples show that in prophetic prayer, the Holy Spirit will take the initiative to direct us in intercession. At other times, we may want to pray about an issue, but not know how to. We can stop, be silent, and ask the Lord how we should pray. As we listen, insight will come. Or, while in prayer, we may hear ourselves say something that takes us by surprise. That is the Holy Spirit injecting prophetic insight into our intercession. We do not have to have a prophetic gift or be a prophet to engage in this type of prayer. When at times we pray prophetically, it will empower us to pray with bold faith, and will add a greater authority to our intercession.

In the next chapter, we will look at something closely connected to prophetic prayer – declaration.

chapter eight

THE POWER OF DECLARATION

Allied with prophetic prayer is declarative prayer, or declaration for short. Once we have heard God speak and we know his will, then not only should we intercede about it, but there comes a time to also declare it. Prayer and declaration are entwined: "You will make your *prayer* to Him. He will hear you...you will also *declare* a thing, and it will be established for you; So light will shine on your ways." [1] To declare something is to make it known, to announce it openly.[2] Prayer is asking for something to happen; declaration is announcing that it will happen. A young girl attended one of our seminars with her mother. On listening to us teach this concept, she turned to her mother and said, "Oh I get it – you don't only pray it, you say it!"

---

[1]   Job 22:27-28 (NKJV) emphasis mine.
[2]   *The Concise Oxford Dictionary*, Oxford, Oxford University Press, 1982

And that is the essence of declaration – we don't only pray it, we also say it.

An Example

For example, Jesus promised that he would build his Church, and all the gates or powers of hell would not conquer it.[3] This is good news in a world that is growing darker by the day, and in which Satan is roaring loudly. When we hear negative global news, we can pray something like this: "Lord Jesus, you promised that you would build your Church and that the powers of hell would not overcome it. Lord, fulfil your word and let it be so. Let your Church grow more and more glorious the darker the world becomes." This is essentially praying that God's kingdom would come to earth, because the Church is his instrument to extend that kingdom.

However, we can also turn this Biblical truth into a declaration or decree:[4] "I declare that Jesus will build his church and the powers of hell will not overcome it. The Church will grow more and more glorious the darker the world becomes." Prayer is vital, but there comes a time to also declare that it will happen. When we authoritatively declare something, our faith level and confidence will increase.

---

[3]   See Matthew 16:18

[4]   Technically, to decree something is to issue an authoritative order, one that has the full force of the law behind it. Declaration and decree are therefore closely connected.

If It's God's Will, Pray and Declare It

As long as something is God's will, we can both pray and declare that it will happen. It's no use declaring something that is not his will, for he will not fulfil it. Many who have embraced extreme faith teaching have mistakenly believed that if they declare it, they can have it. Inevitably, they have been disappointed. If it is a clear promise in the Bible, like the example above, then we can declare it. Alternatively, as we hear God's voice prophetically on a matter, and have it confirmed in one or two other ways,[5] then we can not only intercede for it to happen, but also declare that it will be so.

Sometimes, when you have prayed for something for a long time, the Holy Spirit will give you the assurance that the answer will come. It may then be time to stop praying and simply declare that it will happen, thanking the Lord for the answer. There are no rules around this – it is best to let the Holy Spirit lead us, for he is a very capable teacher.

The Lesson of the Fig Tree

We see this *pray and say it* principle in the Gospel of Mark and the lesson of the fig tree. One time, Jesus cursed a fig tree that should have been laden with fruit but had none. Amazed to see the tree wither from the roots up, the disciples were perplexed. Jesus explained:

---

[5]   For example, a scripture, counsel of others, a sign, circumstances lining up, and so on.

Have faith in God. Truly I tell you, if anyone *says* to this mountain, 'Go, throw yourself into the sea,' and does not doubt in their heart but believes that what they say will happen, it will be done for them. Therefore, I tell you, whatever you *ask* for in prayer, believe that you have received it, and it will be yours. [6]

Ask in prayer…*say* to the mountain. Impossible obstacles move, when we declare that it will be so.

A Miracle Healing

Some years ago, prior to us leaving for an overseas ministry trip, Greta broke her foot. She explains:

In an accident, I fractured one of the short, thick bones in my right mid-foot, with the extra complication of a displaced bone fragment. The orthopedic surgeon sent me home from the Accident and Emergency Department in a plaster cast with crutches, saying that once the inflammation and swelling had settled, I faced an operation involving screws and plates. A lengthy rehabilitation would then follow. He also warned me that I would be unlikely to run anymore, something I love to do. I was facing a personal mountain.

---

[6]   Mark 11:22-24 (NIV), emphasis mine.

We contacted a few close friends and asked them to pray with us for a miracle. I spent much time with the Lord, worshipping him in spite of my dilemma, and praying for supernatural healing. The Holy Spirit repeatedly brought Mark 11:22-24 to mind. So I simply did what Jesus instructed.

First I prayed, "Lord, I ask that you will put the bone fragment back in place and that there will be no fracture. I believe I have received it; I receive it now. It is mine." Then I declared out loud, "I say to this mountain of foot injury, go! Bone fragment, go back into place now. I declare that there is no fracture. In Jesus' Name I decree a perfect X-ray."

A few days later, I returned to the surgeon and audaciously requested another X-ray. In the natural, this was a pointless exercise so soon after the first one, as the image would be unchanged. Surprisingly, he agreed and immediately ordered a sophisticated scan. A few hours later I picked up the report. With bated breath I opened it. It read, "There is no sign of a displaced bone fragment. There is no sign of a fracture. No abnormality detected." Within a week, God had moved an impossible mountain as I declared his word over my foot.

If we know something is God's will, and have prayed for it to happen, then declaration often releases the answer. Greta and I, along with our friends, rejoiced in the miracle God had worked, and we were able to fly overseas as planned.

Change Your Words

Pastor Tak Bhana, senior leader of Church Unlimited in New Zealand, writes about the power of declaration:

> Change your words and change your world! Words are powerful, especially when they echo God's word, or repeat prophetic words he has spoken to us. Making declarations has been one of the greatest keys to my life and ministry, and a powerful way to experience breakthroughs. We're introduced to this principle in Genesis 1:2-3 (NKJV): "The earth was without form, and void; and darkness was on the face of the deep. And the Spirit of God was hovering over the face of the waters. Then God said, 'Let there be light,' and there was light." The darkness remained until God declared, "Let there be light."
>
> Years ago, my wife Adrienne, an avid walker, experienced severe pain in her feet. One night, I laid my hands on her feet and as I prayed, Luke 10:19 (NKJV) came to mind: "I give you the authority to trample on serpents and scorpions, and over all the power of the enemy, and nothing shall by any means hurt you." I declared that verse as I prayed, and soon her feet were healed. Throughout the Bible, God speaks things into being: "God, who gives life to the dead and calls those things which do not exist as though they did." [7]
>
> Change your words; change your world!

---

[7]   Romans 4:17b (NKJV)

Praying and declaring God's word – whether it be a genuine prophecy or a scripture – can change not only our immediate world, but the world at large. In the next chapter, we will look more specifically at the impact of praying God's written word.

chapter nine

PRAYING SCRIPTURE

It was a shock. I had discovered a lump in my groin, and on examining it, my doctor suspected that it may be malignant, and ordered a biopsy. Sometime later, I nervously made my way to hospital, checked in, and was escorted to a bed. While awaiting the procedure, I opened my Bible to Psalm 41, directed there by my daily reading guide. The first few verses arrested me: "Blessed are those who have regard for the weak; the Lord delivers them in times of trouble. The Lord protects and preserves them…The Lord sustains them on their sickbed and restores them from their bed of illness." [1] How incredible that of all the words in the Bible, those were the ones I read that day.

Soon after the biopsy, the oncologist gave Jane and me the news. I had Hodgkin's disease, a type of cancer of the lymphatic system. It had infected my chest, neck, and groin. "There's an eighty percent chance of recovery with chemotherapy," he explained, "and treatment will start in a few weeks."

---

[1]   Psalm 41:1-3 (NIV)

I was thirty-one at the time. Nine long months of chemotherapy followed, and during those months, fear and depression often assaulted me.

However, we had a powerful scripture that God had gifted to us. So we regularly prayed that his word would come true: "Lord you promised to protect and preserve me, to deliver me in times of trouble. You said that you would sustain me in sickness and restore me to health. We believe for a hundred percent recovery. Lord, fulfil your word to us." When times were especially dark, we would make the following declaration: "Lord you will protect and preserve me, and deliver me in this time of trouble. You will sustain me in sickness and restore me to health. There will be a hundred percent recovery. Thank you that you will fulfil your word to us."

Finally, the nine months of chemotherapy ended. The doctors pronounced me in remission. In fact, I have been healed of the disease ever since, because on a hospital bed one morning, God promised to "restore me from my bed of illness." I discovered that praying scripture releases faith and authority unlike anything else. "Faith comes when you hear God speak to you," wrote the apostle Paul.[2] A prophecy, vision, or dream from God carries authority and is powerful ammunition for prayer. But a scripture made alive by the Holy Spirit carries a super-authority, because the written word is God-breathed and utterly reliable.[3]

---

[2]   Romans 10:17 paraphrased
[3]   See 2 Timothy 3:16

Ammunition for Prayer

As long as we are certain that God has revealed the right scripture for the situation, then we can turn that scripture into prayer or declaration that will greatly impact the spiritual realm. As one preacher said, "Prayer is like a gun; faith is the barrel; the name of Jesus is the trigger; and scripture is the bullet." Often, God reveals scriptures to us but we do little with them, except perhaps to record them in journals that gather dust on a bookshelf. It's like filling the magazine of a rifle with bullets, but never putting the magazine into the weapon. We need to fire the bullets.

"So also will be the word that I speak:" declares God to Isaiah the prophet, "it does not return to me unfulfilled. My word performs my purpose and fulfils the mission I sent it out to accomplish." [4] The Bible is a treasure trove of truth that we can employ in prayer. Some verses are instantly available for prayer if we know where to look. Others we need to seek God for. If we routinely read the Bible, God may quicken a scripture to us for ourselves, others, or the situation, city, or nation that we are praying for. To *quicken* means to rouse, inspire, burn brighter, come to life. [5]

When God does this, we need to not only believe the verse or verses, but pray them back to him, so that he will accomplish it. To use another military analogy, when we pray scripture, that truth goes out into the spiritual realm like a guided missile searching for a stronghold to destroy. Praying and declaring Psalm 41 certainly prevented fear from becoming a stronghold

---

4   Isaiah 55:11 (TPT)
5   *The Concise Oxford Dictionary*, Oxford, Oxford University Press, 1982

in my mind when I battled cancer.

Alternatively, while praying, a scripture may come to mind that is a specific word for the situation we are interceding about. The scripture may shed light on the situation and show us how to pray. Or it may predict something that Satan is planning, so that we can pray that it does not occur.

A Financial Breakthrough

A few years ago, when our ministry finances were unusually low, Greta and I prayed for provision. As we did, the following Bible verse came to mind: "And God is able to provide you with every blessing in abundance, so that you may always have enough of everything and may provide in abundance for every good work." [6] After giving a gift to another travelling ministry as a seed, we began to pray and declare this encouraging promise from God. We also resisted any spirit of lack from the devil that would try and restrict the flow of finance to us. We prayed that we would have not *just enough*, but *more than enough* to do God's work.

After a few weeks, a breakthrough came and finance began to flow from unlikely sources, and it has kept coming ever since. This has enabled us to minister in places that could not afford to pay much, and give finance away to other organisations, especially those that help the poor. Something broke around that time, because of the power of praying and declaring a scripture remarkably applicable to our circumstances.

---

[6]   2 Corinthians 9:8 (RSV)

In whatever way we receive the scripture – whether in reading the Bible or as an impression while in prayer – we should pray it regularly and persist until it happens. If we do, the entire Godhead of Father, Son, and Holy Spirit will work to fulfil it.

A Compelling Scripture to Pray

The apostle Paul's prayer for the Ephesian church is one of the most magnificent prayers in all the Bible. It is a powerful prayer, not merely for one church, but for all believers everywhere and in every age. It is the Father's will for all his sons and daughters. It begins, "I pray that from his glorious unlimited resources, God will give you mighty inner strength through his Holy Spirit," and continues in the most sublime way. It can become our own prayer by simply changing *you* to *me*. It then reads:

> Father, I pray that from your glorious, unlimited resources you will give me mighty inner strength through your Holy Spirit. And I pray that Christ will be more and more at home in my heart as I trust in him. May my roots go down deep into the soil of your marvellous love. And may I have the power to understand, as all God's people should, how wide, how long, how high, and how deep your love really is.
>
> May I experience the love of Christ, though it is so great I will never fully understand it. Then I will be filled with the fullness of life and power that comes from you. Now glory be to God!

By your mighty power at work within me, you are able to accomplish infinitely more than I would ever dare to ask or hope. [7]

Try it, not only for yourself, but for others you care about. Greta and I pray this for ourselves, our children, grandchildren, and future descendants at least weekly. It is a prayer that the Father longs to answer. We don't have to wait for him to quicken it to us – it is the indisputable will of God for all his children.

Regular reading of the entire Bible – many reading guides are available on the internet to help read the Bible through in a year – will help us become familiar with the many such prayers and promises that pepper scripture. It is vital that we have heaven's viewpoint in a world spiralling increasingly downwards. Psalm 2, for example, is fast becoming a blueprint for both current and future world events. Praying through it will give great insight on how to intercede for nations and governments at this time.[8]

God's Word Energises Prayer

According to the book of Hebrews, "The word of God is living and active *and* full of power, making it operative, energizing, and effective." [9] The richer we are in God's word, the richer we will be in prayer. Praying scripture will help energise our prayer lives. A writer, whose name is lost to history, once said of the Bible:

---

[7]   Adapted from Ephesians 3:16-20
[8]   For more explanation, see my blog on this at www.spiritlife.org.nz/blog.
[9]   Hebrews 4:12a (AMP)

This Book is the mind of God, the state of man, the way of salvation, the doom of sinners, and the happiness of believers. Its doctrines are holy, its precepts are binding; its histories are true, and its decisions are immutable. Read it to be wise, believe it to be safe, practice it to be holy. It contains light to direct you, food to support you, and comfort to cheer you.

It is the traveller's map, the pilgrim's staff, the pilot's compass, the soldier's sword, and the Christian's character. Here paradise is restored, heaven opened, and the gates of hell disclosed. Christ is its grand subject, our good its design, and the glory of God its end. It should fill the memory, rule the heart, and guide the feet.

Read it slowly, frequently, prayerfully. It is a mine of wealth, a paradise of glory, and a river of pleasure. Follow its precepts and it will lead you to Calvary, to the empty tomb, to a resurrected life in Christ; yes, to glory itself, for eternity.[10]

Praying scripture releases greater faith and authority within us, both being important conditions for answered prayer. In the next chapter, we will discuss another very effective tool that God has given to help us pray.

---

[10]   www.sermonillustrations.com/a-z/b/bible_value_of.htm, accessed 28/08/2021

chapter ten

PRAYING IN TONGUES

It happened on the very first day. At the time I didn't realise that it would change the course of my life. Fresh out of high school, I had come to Christchurch, New Zealand's largest southern city, to study chemistry at Canterbury University. Settling in to my room at Rochester Hall, a university hall of residence, I was dismayed to discover that the kitchen would not be serving meals for the first week, until the start of lectures. *Oh well,* I thought to myself, *there are takeaway places nearby.* Then he appeared — a tall, friendly young man with curly hair and a big smile. Mike was a fellow resident of Rochester Hall.

"Some of my friends have a flat nearby and are inviting people over for dinner. Would you like to come?" I jumped at the thought of a free meal and, together with two other students, accompanied Mike to the house. The flatmates — all fellow students — had put on a nice dinner which we enjoyed over pleasant conversation. *These Canterbury students are very friendly and kind* I mused inwardly. Over the coming days, Mike, a senior student, continued to help with any questions

I had about university life. Sometime later, he invited me to a weekly Bible discussion group that he was hosting in his room. I agreed to attend, feeling that it was the least I could do after all his kindness to me.

During the rest of the year, I and a number of others attended the group. While some were sceptical as we discussed the Gospel of John, I both believed in God and accepted the Bible as his word, due to my church upbringing. But I had no real relationship with God. It was early the following year that I finally realised why Jesus Christ had died on the cross and how I needed to be born again spiritually. Jesus said; "I tell you the truth, unless you are born again, you cannot see the Kingdom of God." [1] So I gave my life to Christ and made him my Lord from that time on.

I discovered that Mike and his friends belonged to *The Navigators*, a Christian ministry making disciples on university campuses and in other places around the world. Mike taught me to have a daily time with God in prayer and Bible reading, to study the Bible, and to memorise scripture. He is now in heaven, but I remain deeply thankful for all the help he gave me at the start of my Christian life.

Something Is Missing

Over the next two years, my life became spiritually regimented: daily quiet times (as we called Bible reading and prayer), weekly Bible study, and lots of scripture memorisation. I also led a Bible

---

[1]   John 3:3

discussion group, which some fellow students attended. In terms of having a disciplined Christian life, I excelled. And yet as time went by, I increasingly felt that something was missing – all my disciplines began to feel like empty routine.

It was during a holiday break in my hometown of Blenheim, north of Christchurch, that I ran into one of my old high school teachers. Knowing that he was a Christian, I told him that I had become a believer. He invited me to his home, where he and his wife listened eagerly as I explained all that had happened to me. "But I feel that something is missing," I concluded.

"What you need is to be baptised in the Holy Spirit," they replied.

"But I was baptised as a baby."

"We're not talking about water baptism, but another baptism – being filled with the Holy Spirit."

Over the next half an hour they explained from the Bible exactly what this was – an experience after conversion [2] that empowered a believer to live for Christ, operate in the supernatural gifts of the Spirit, and be a witness for Jesus. The more they spoke, the more I desired this experience. Finally, I exclaimed, "I want it!" Right there and then, they placed their hands on my head and prayed that Jesus would baptise me with

---

[2] In Acts 10:43-46 a Roman army officer named Cornelius and his family and friends were baptised in the Spirit simultaneously with their conversion to Christ. All other instances of Holy Spirit baptism in the Book of Acts occur after people's conversions.

his Holy Spirit.[3] I felt the Spirit's presence come over me, and power well up within me, flooding my soul with joy and peace. [4]

"Now we will pray that you speak in tongues, for it is one of the gifts God gives to those baptised with his Holy Spirit."

After explaining what this was, they again prayed for me, but due to my self-consciousness, I stifled any attempt to speak in some strange new prayer language. They told me to go home and spend time with God and the gift would come. As I drove home, I knew something profound had happened – I felt so overcome with God's joy and love that it was hard to concentrate on driving!

That night, in my bedroom, I asked God to give me the gift of tongues. A moment later, the sound *la* came into my head, and as I spoke it out, a torrent of non-English words poured out of me. That one syllable, spoken in faith, was like the starter motor of a whole new language. Afraid to stop speaking in tongues in case I couldn't start again, I continued until I finally fell asleep. The next morning, I discovered that the gift was still there and that I could speak in tongues at will. And when I had my quiet time, reading the Bible was completely different – I encountered Jesus in its pages like never before. "The Bible is Jesus in print," said one pastor, and that is what I was experiencing.

---

[3]   The terms baptism *in, with,* and *of* the Holy Spirit are used interchangeably throughout this chapter.

[4]   See Acts 1:8: "But you will receive power when the Holy Spirit *comes upon* you. And you will be my witnesses, telling people about me everywhere..." and John 7:38-39: "Anyone who believes in me may come and drink! For the Scriptures declare, 'Rivers of living water will *flow from his heart.*' (When he said 'living water', he was speaking of the Spirit.)"

Prayer, too, seemed much easier. Before, I had felt obligated to read the Bible and pray – now I wanted to.

A week later, I was baptised in the Wairau River by the pastor of the Elim Church, which my teacher friend and his wife attended. As I came up out of the icy waters, the Spirit came upon me again, and I spoke very loudly in tongues. And I have spoken in tongues ever since. It is not within the scope of this book to discuss the baptism of the Holy Spirit in detail – there are many good books on the subject.[5] But it is appropriate to discuss what speaking in tongues is, and how it can be an extremely effective tool in prayer.

What is Speaking in Tongues?

There are nine gifts of the Holy Spirit listed by the apostle Paul, and the ability to speak in tongues is one of them.[6] In his great discourse on love, Paul says, "If I speak in the tongues of men and of angels, but have not love, I am a noisy gong or a clanging cymbal."[7] In other words, love must be supreme in all that we do, and all supernatural power is meaningless without love. Note the description of tongues though – it is the language of humans and angels. That is, speaking in tongues may be speaking in an earthly language unknown to the speaker, or it may be speaking in a heavenly language unknown on earth.

---

[5]   One of the classics is *Nine O'clock in the Morning*, by Dennis J Bennet.
[6]   See 1 Corinthians 12:8-10 (NKJV paraphrased): the word of wisdom, the word of knowledge, faith, healings, miracles, discerning of spirits, prophecy, speaking in tongues, and the interpretation of tongues.
[7]   1 Corinthians 13:1 (RSV)

We see an example of the first on Pentecost Day when Jesus' disciples were baptised in the Holy Spirit and began to speak in tongues.[8] "At that time there were devout Jews from every nation living in Jerusalem," records the Book of Acts. "When they heard the loud noise, everyone came running, and they were bewildered to hear their own languages being spoken by the believers. They were completely amazed. 'How can this be?' they exclaimed. 'These people are all from Galilee, and yet… we all hear these people speaking in our own languages about the wonderful things God has done!' " [9]

Many years ago, a friend of mine visited the underground church in China. Attending a house church meeting, he listened to the attendees' fervent worship and prayer. Then, two elderly ladies spoke out in flawless English. Turning to the house church leader, he asked how they knew English so well. The leader replied, "They cannot speak any English. They were speaking in tongues."

Regarding a heavenly language, no one knows all of the many thousands of languages and dialects on earth, so we could probably not tell if someone was speaking in an angelic language. But if the Bible mentions it, then it must happen. In summary then, the gift of tongues is the Holy Spirit enabling a person to speak in an earthly or heavenly language unknown to that speaker. But what is the gift for?

---

[8]   See Acts 2:1-4 (NIV)
[9]   Acts 2:5-8a, 11b

What is Speaking in Tongues For?

There are two distinct ways that tongues can operate. First, tongues, like prophecy, may be an encouraging message in a church or home meeting, where it needs the gift of interpretation as well. Paul, when instructing the Corinthian church on how to have well-ordered meetings, says of tongues, "No more than two or three should speak in tongues. They must speak one at a time, and someone must interpret what they say. But if no one is present who can interpret, they must be silent in your church meeting and speak in tongues to God privately." [10]

Interpretation, being a gift of the Spirit, does not require understanding of the language spoken in tongues. Someone interprets a message in tongues by speaking out in faith the meaning as the Holy Spirit inspires them – it's an interpretation, not necessarily a word-for-word translation. Tongues and interpretation in a meeting is God communicating to the church. In this setting, Paul is clear that not all will speak in tongues. [11] But note that he says if a person shouldn't speak in tongues in a meeting, then they can do it in private. Which leads to the second way that tongues can be used.

Speaking in tongues can also be prayer and praise to God by an individual in private, or a group doing it simultaneously. [12] Paul valued this use of the gift so highly that he said, "I thank God that I speak in tongues more than any of you." [13]

---

[10]   1 Corinthians 14:27-28
[11]   See 1 Corinthians 12:30
[12]   For simultaneous use of this gift by a group, see Acts 2:4, Acts 10:44-46, and Acts 19:6.
[13]   1 Corinthians 14:18

Whereas public use of the gift in a meeting is *God speaking to people*, the private use of tongues is *people speaking to God*, and doesn't need interpretation.

What Happens When We Speak in Tongues?

When we pray, worship, or praise in tongues, something amazing happens. Not only do we strengthen ourselves spiritually,[14] but we communicate with God in a perfect way. What is one of the biggest hindrances to prayer? It's being unsure that we are praying in God's will. When we pray with the mind, we may battle a lack of knowledge, difficulty in expressing ourselves, or prejudices that affect how we pray. These can be overcome as we mature, but praying in tongues instantly overcomes them, allowing us to pray in the perfect will of God.

Here's how it happens: "No one can know a person's thoughts except that person's own spirit," says the Bible.[15] Our spirit is the innermost part of our being and truly knows us, whereas our conscious mind doesn't. For example, we may be surprised at some of the things we say or do, asking, "Why am I like this?" But our spirit knows and understands us. "The human spirit," writes King Solomon, "is the lamp of the Lord that sheds light on one's inmost being." [16] In a similar way, the Holy Spirit knows and understands God completely.

---

[14]   See 1 Corinthians 14:4: "One who speaks in a tongue is strengthened personally…"
[15]   1 Corinthians 2:11a
[16]   Proverbs 20:27 (NIV)

"The Spirit searches all things, even the deep things of God," writes Paul.[17] All things includes our spirit. The Holy Spirit searches and understands both our spirit and God. If we can then join our spirit with the Spirit of God, effective prayer will result. *This happens when we pray in tongues.* "If I pray in tongues," says Paul, "my spirit is praying."[18] The Holy Spirit enables our spirit to unite with him in prayer or praise to God.

When we pray in tongues for ourselves or others, the Holy Spirit communicates to the Father and Jesus our exact needs and desires, or the true need concerning a situation in the world. When we praise or worship in tongues, the Holy Spirit perfectly expresses the adoration that our spirit feels for God and which we can't express fully through our minds.

When Jesus returns and establishes his kingdom, the gifts of the Spirit will cease: "As for prophecies, they will pass away; as for tongues, they will cease; as for knowledge, it will pass away."[19] Note, however, the next verse: "For our knowledge is imperfect and our prophecy is imperfect."[20] No mention is made of tongues being imperfect. Though it is a temporary gift that we will no longer need in the age to come, it is perfect prayer and praise to God.

---

[17] 1 Corinthians 2:10 (NIV)
[18] 1 Corinthians 14:14a
[19] 1 Corinthians 13:8 (RSV)
[20] 1 Corinthians 13:9 (RSV)

A Problem

There is a problem, however, when we speak in tongues. "For anyone who speaks in a tongue," writes Paul, "does not speak to people but to God. Indeed, no one understands them; they utter mysteries by the Spirit." [21] Praying in tongues is not only mysterious to anyone hearing it, but also to the speaker: "For if I pray in tongues, my spirit is praying, but I don't understand what I am saying." [22] This means that our mind may wander when praying or worshipping in tongues.

What's the answer to this problem? Addressing this issue, Paul advises, "Well then, what shall I do? I will pray in the spirit and I will also pray in words I understand. I will sing in the spirit, and I will also sing in words I understand." [23] The answer is to intersperse prayer in our native tongue with prayer in tongues. Throughout my prayer times, I mix praying in English and praying in tongues. Sometimes as we pray, praise, or sing in tongues, we may have a general sense of what we are saying. This in turn allows us to pray in our natural language with clearer direction and greater anointing.

At other times, when praying for a certain issue, the sound of the tongues may even change. The Holy Spirit is not limited to one spiritual language. Others even suggest that if we pray in tongues, we can ask the Lord for the interpretation, and then by faith pray out in our normal language. I have tried this occasionally and been surprised by the higher level of prayer that has come out of my mouth.

---

[21]   1 Corinthians 14:2 (NIV)
[22]   1 Corinthians 14:14
[23]   1 Corinthians 14:15

But What If I Can't Speak in Tongues?

Not everyone who reads this will speak in tongues. That should not discourage us. Praying in our native language as the Holy Spirit inspires us, engaging in prophetic prayer and declaration, praying scripture, and praying through the Lord's Prayer – all these are powerful forms of prayer and should make up the majority of our prayer lives. But if we can speak in tongues, it will add a very valuable tool to assist us in prayer.

Signs should accompany the baptism of the Spirit, and these signs are usually the immediate or subsequent release of the gifts of the Spirit through us, including tongues. If we ask God for it, he will grant us the gift of tongues. Jesus said, "And these signs will follow those who believe: In My name they will cast out demons; they will speak with new tongues." [24] Nearly four centuries later, Saint Augustine,[25] in his book *City of God*, wrote, "We still do what the apostles did when they laid hands on the Samaritans and called down the Holy Spirit on them by laying on of hands. It is expected that converts should speak with new tongues."

How to Receive the Baptism of the Spirit and Tongues

As with salvation, there is an ABC of receiving the baptism of the Holy Spirit with tongues. To be saved, we *asked* God to forgive our sins, *believed* that Jesus died for us and rose again from the dead, and *confessed* publicly that we were now

---

[24] Mark 16:17 (NKJV)
[25] Saint Augustine, 354-430.

Christians. In the same way, we *ask* that Jesus would baptise us
with the Holy Spirit. Spiritual hunger and tenacity is important
here – some people are filled with the Spirit as soon as they ask,
others may have to persevere.

Then we need to *believe* that what we ask for will happen.
Speaking to the people of his day, Jesus promised, "So if you
sinful people know how to give good gifts to your children,
how much more will your heavenly Father give the Holy Spirit
to those who ask him." [26] God is eager to fill us with his Spirit.
Remember that if you are a believer you already have the Holy
Spirit living within you. [27] In the baptism of the Spirit, he
comes upon you in power and flows out of you like a river to
bless others.

Finally, we need to *confess* that we are filled. We do this
not with our natural language, but with tongues. [28] As you ask
and believe to be baptised in the Spirit, fix your eyes on Jesus,
let him fill you, and desire to praise him in tongues. The Holy
Spirit will put the first sound or syllable of a new language on
your tongue or in the speech centre of your brain. As you speak
it out in faith, more will come.

Having someone pray for us helps, but you can receive
on your own. Like me, Greta became a follower of Christ at
university. During the holiday break a few months later, she read

---

[26]   Luke 11:13
[27]   See Romans 8:9b (NLT 1996 version): "Those who do not have the Spirit
        of Christ living in them are not Christians at all."
[28]   In a more general sense, a sign of the baptism of the Spirit is prophetic
        speech. See Acts 19: 1-7 where they both prophesied and spoke in tongues
        when filled.

a book on the baptism in the Holy Spirit. No one was nearby to pray for her, so she just asked the Lord to do it. Straightaway, she was filled with the Spirit and began to speak in tongues.

If you desire to be baptised with the Holy Spirit, here is a suggested prayer that you can use if you are on your own:

> Dear Heavenly Father, in the name of Jesus Christ, I renounce all my sins and especially any involvement in the occult. I renounce all fear and unbelief and any blockage of my mind. I ask you Lord Jesus to baptise me with the Holy Spirit. Let your Spirit come upon me and let rivers of living water flow out of me. Lord Jesus, I receive this now. Please also give me the gift of speaking in tongues.

Pray this and expect to receive. If nothing happens, then it could indicate that the Lord wants you to ask someone to pray for you. Be persistent until it happens. Having said that, I know many fine Christians who do not speak in tongues and their prayer lives are powerful and effective. Speaking in tongues is not a badge of spirituality – it's simply a tool to help us pray. And I want every tool in the toolkit in order to pray and change my world.

In the next chapter, we will look at another tool that is within reach of everyone – fasting.

chapter eleven

PRAYER AND FASTING: POTENT DUO

I like food. My four grandparents immigrated to New Zealand from Bsharri, a village located in the northern mountains of Lebanon. The region is renowned for its hospitality, especially around food. My mother was a superb cook and I grew up on a diet of tasty Lebanese and European meals. On special occasions, the dining table groaned under the weight of the delicious dishes placed on it. This trained me to like food. Have I mentioned that I like food? So I don't find fasting easy, but I do find fasting necessary.

What is Fasting?

Fasting is abstaining from food, or other pleasures, for spiritual purposes. Fasting is not a diet, and is of little value without prayer.[1] As one pastor put it, "When prayer is connected with fasting, it's like a neon sign in the spiritual realm flashing the words 'I am serious.' " Fasting demonstrates to God that we are hungrier for him than we are for our food. Fasting is not for a zealous few, but is to be a regular discipline for every Christian, like prayer, reading the Bible, attending church, and giving.

Straight after teaching about prayer in his Sermon on the Mount,[2] and revealing the Lord's Prayer as a pattern to follow, Jesus mentioned fasting. "When you fast," he said, "don't look gloomy and pretend to be spiritual...don't let it be obvious, but instead, wash your face and groom yourself and realise that your Father in the secret place is the one who is watching all that you do in secret and will continue to reward you."[3] Jesus warned against fasting out of pride to feel spiritually superior to others. Fasting is a way to humble, not exalt, ourselves.[4] It's wise not to tell others that you are fasting, unless you are part of a group doing it together. Do it in secret if possible. Note Jesus' use of the word *when* in these verses. When you fast, not *if* you fast.

Jesus expects his followers to fast, but not as some compulsory discipline to deprive us of the joy of life. Instead, it's a way in which a kind heavenly Father can bless and reward his children. Consistent fasting brings consistent rewards. The rewards aren't the main reason we fast. Rather, it is seeking God himself, to draw closer to him. God is so generous, however, that he can't help but reward us. "Without faith it is impossible

---

[1]   There are health benefits from fasting, and you may lose weight too. But these are not the primary reasons why we fast.
[2]   See Matthew 5-7
[3]   Matthew 6:16-18 (TPT)
[4]   See Psalm 35:13 (NIV): "I ...humbled myself with fasting."

to please God," declares the Bible, "because anyone who comes to him must believe that he exists and that he rewards those who earnestly seek him." [5] Fasting shows God that we are earnest.

Fasting in the Early Church

"But the disciples didn't fast, they feasted," someone may say. True, while Jesus was with them, their feasting was so noticeable that the religious Jews, who fasted twice a week, complained about it. Jesus replied to them, "Do wedding guests fast while celebrating with the groom? Of course not. They can't fast while the groom is with them. But someday the groom will be taken away from them, and then they will fast." [6] The groom was taken away when Jesus ascended into heaven. When he returns to earth to marry his bride, the perfected Church, there will be a great wedding feast. The Book of Revelation states, "For the time has come for the wedding feast of the Lamb, and his bride has prepared herself. She has been given the finest of pure white linen to wear... And the angel said to me, 'Write this: Blessed are those who are invited to the wedding feast of the Lamb.' " [7] At that time fasting will cease; until then the Church will fast.

We see this in the early Church: "Now in the church at Antioch there were prophets and teachers... While they were worshiping the Lord and fasting, the Holy Spirit said, 'Set apart for me Barnabas and Saul for the work to which I have called them.' So after they had fasted and prayed, they placed their

---

[5]   Hebrews 11:6 (NIV)
[6]   Mark 2:19-20
[7]   Revelation 19:7b-9a

hands on them and sent them off." [8] Group fasting and prayer by the leaders of the Antioch church, caused two apostles to emerge – Saul (later called Paul) and Barnabas – who took the gospel into Asia and Europe. In the same way, the great missional movements of the last days will also come out of fasting and prayer, especially by church leaders.

In having to defend his apostolic ministry to the Corinthian church, Paul lists his attributes as a true apostle. One of those attributes was *in fastings often.*[9] And fasting didn't stop when all the apostles died. Church tradition and history reveal that for several centuries, the early Church fasted on Wednesday and Friday of each week. Throughout the centuries, spiritual movements that changed nations practised fasting. For example, Bible teacher Derek Prince[10] writes, "The early Methodists… regularly practised fasting…John Wesley would not ordain a man to the Methodist ministry unless he would commit himself to fast every Wednesday and Friday until 4pm. In other words, Wesley regarded it as an absolutely normal part of any Christian minister's life and discipline."[11]

But What if I Can't Fast?

Some people can't fast. Breast-feeding mothers, a parent taking care of very young children, or those with jobs involving heavy manual labour, may find it difficult to fast. If a person has

[8]   Acts 13:1a, 2-3 (NIV)
[9]   2 Corinthians 11:27 (NKJV)
[10]   Derek Prince, 1915-2003
[11]   Derek Prince, *How to Fast Successfully*, New Kensington, Whitaker House, 1976, p.17

a medical condition, is ill, or is taking medication, then they should ask their doctor if it's safe for them to fast. For example, it would not be wise for someone with diabetes to fast.

But all is not lost. In Bible times, food, family, friends, and work were the main stimuli in a person's life. That's why Jesus taught about fasting from food and getting alone with God to pray. Today, we have many other stimuli, such as television, smart phones, the internet, social media, You Tube and so on. If we're not able to fast from food, then perhaps we can put some of these other things aside for a time to seek God. "We have to get off Facebook," quipped one pastor, "and seek God's Face and get into his Book."

Theologian James Packer [12] writes:

> We tend to think of fasting as going without food. But we can fast from anything. If we love music and decide to miss a concert in order to spend time with God, that is fasting. It is helpful to think of the parallel of human friendship. When friends need to be together, they will cancel all other activities in order to make that possible. There's nothing magical about fasting. It's just one way of telling God that your priority at that moment is to be alone with him…and you have cancelled the meal, party, concert, or whatever else you had planned to do in order to fulfil that priority.[13]

---

[12]   J. I. Packer, 1926-2020
[13]   J.I. Packer, *Your Father Loves You*, Wheaton, Harold Shaw Publishers, 1986, p. 14.

Benefits of Fasting

There are many benefits of fasting but it is not within the scope of this book to discuss them all. Here are some:

Fasting brings a spiritual sharpness.

Fasting allows us to hear God's voice more clearly.

Fasting brings greater closeness to the Lord.

Fasting enhances the power of prayer.

Fasting increases anointing for vocation, ministry, and service.

Fasting releases miracles.

Fasting overcomes human and demonic resistance to breakthrough.

The following incident in ancient Israel illustrates the power of fasting. The depraved men of Gibeah, a village located within the tribe of Benjamin, had raped and killed the concubine of a Levite. The Levite reported this crime to the other eleven tribes who then sent messengers to Benjamin's leaders, ordering them to hand over the guilty men for execution. They refused, so after inquiring of God, the rest of Israel went to fight against Benjamin. In the first battle, the Israelites lost twenty-two thousand men.

After this shock defeat, they returned to camp and wept until evening, a picture of not only grief, but also prayer. In the second skirmish the next day, they lost another eighteen thousand men. The Bible records their response to this further devastating loss: "Then all the Israelites went up to Bethel and wept in the presence of the Lord and fasted until evening." [14] The next day, they went into battle again, and this time, they completely routed the Benjaminites.

What made the difference? Fasting. Jesus confirmed this when he told the disciples why they could not cast a demonic spirit out of a mute boy with epilepsy. "This kind," explained Jesus, "can be cast out only by prayer and fasting." [15] Some miracles and breakthroughs only come when we add fasting to prayer. Some people don't get saved unless we fast and pray for them. In *Fasting*,[16] one of the best books on the subject, Pastor Jentezen Franklin shares many miracles and breakthroughs obtained by prayer and fasting.

How to Fast

In a *complete fast*, no food is eaten. If it's a shorter fast, people might drink only water, and it is good to drink frequently to stay hydrated. In longer fasts, people may also drink juice or vegetable broth, to give themselves some energy. Then there is the *partial fast*, where we abstain from meat, refined carbohydrates, alcohol, sugary foods and drinks, or other rich food. The prophet Daniel fasted partially for three weeks, and

---

[14]   Judges 20:26a
[15]   Mark 9:29
[16]   Jentezen Franklin, *Fasting*, Lake Mary, Charisma House, 2014

the Bible records him as saying, "All that time I had eaten no rich food. No meat or wine crossed my lips." [17]

The key is to decide beforehand what we will do and stick to it, lest the devil tempt us to break our fast prematurely. Once we have decided what we will fast from, we then need to decide how long to fast.

One-Day Fasts

The one-day fast is most common and is very effective if done regularly, for example, weekly. In a one-day fast, we can skip one, two, or all three meals. Greta and I usually fast from after dinner the evening before, skipping breakfast and lunch the next day, and breaking our fast with a light meal in the evening. This works for us and is roughly a twenty-four hour fast. During the day, we have three times of prayer: one in the morning separately, one around lunchtime together, and a final "soaking" time late afternoon, again separately, where we don't intercede but worship the Lord, listening to worship songs and resting in his presence. Often, at that time, he may give us a vision, or speak to us in some way.

Others will have a different pattern to their day – it's important to discover the rhythm of prayer that works for you and not copy someone else. We work from home, so our rhythm is achievable. If you work in an office, for example, then you may have to adapt to your environment. The important thing is to get some time of prayer in the day.

---

[17]   Daniel 10:3

Or even consider taking some leave for an important fast, so that you can spend extra time in prayer.

Three-Day Fasts

Three-day fasts occur three times in the Bible and are exceptionally powerful.

The first time is in the Book of Esther. The Persian Prime Minister Haman had tricked King Xerxes into agreeing to his evil plot to kill all Jews throughout the empire on a certain day. Unbeknown to Haman, and even Xerxes, Queen Esther was a Jew. On learning of the plot, she instructed her uncle Mordecai and other Jews to fast and pray for three days for deliverance. This was a life or death situation. "Go and gather together all the Jews of Susa and fast for me," said Esther. "Do not eat or drink for three days, night or day. My maids and I will do the same. And then, though it is against the law, I will go in to see the king. If I must die, I must die." [18]

This was a total fast, even excluding liquids. Abstaining from liquids is dangerous and not generally recommended unless led by God, and then only for a short time. They fasted and prayed, Esther appealed to King Xerxes, and the tables were completely turned on Haman. The king executed him, and permitted the Jews to defend themselves and kill their enemies. Three days of prayer and fasting had brought total deliverance and a complete reversal of the threat. To this day, Jews celebrate the festival of Purim, celebrating this great event. When we, our family, or

---

[18]   Esther 4:16

nation, face similar onslaughts of evil, a three-day fast, done at regular intervals if necessary, will help turn the tide.

The second occurrence of a three-day fast is in the Book of Ezra. King Artaxerxes of Persia permitted Ezra, a Jewish priest, to take money and other treasures back to Jerusalem to help re-establish the sacrificial system of worship at the reconstructed temple. Before Ezra and his entourage set out for Jerusalem, they paused to check who was in the group, and to fast for three days. Ezra records, "I assembled the exiles at the Ahava Canal, and we camped there for three days while I went over the lists of the people and the priests who had arrived." [19]

He goes on to say, "And there by the Ahava Canal, I gave orders for all of us to fast and humble ourselves before our God. We prayed that he would give us a safe journey and protect us, our children, and our goods as we travelled." [20] Similarly, if we face an important trip, a relocation to another city or nation, or any other major change, it may be wise to fast and pray for three days for protection over us, our children, and our property.

The third occurrence of a three-day fast is in the Book of Acts. In a blinding vision, Jesus appeared to Saul, the vicious persecutor of the early Church, and instructed him to go into the city of Damascus and wait for further instructions. "He remained there blind for three days and did not eat or drink," records the Bible. [21] Meanwhile, the Lord appeared to a disciple named Ananias and said, "Go over to Straight Street, to the house of Judas. When you get there, ask for a man from Tarsus

---

[19]   Ezra 8:15
[20]   Ezra 8:21
[21]   Acts 9:9

named Saul. He is praying to me right now." [22] Ananias went to Saul, and prayed for him. Saul not only received his sight back, but was baptised in the Holy Spirit as well.[23]

This event launched Saul into a ministry that would become one of the most effective of the early Church era. Saul became the apostle Paul, one of the greatest Christians of all time. During his three days of fasting and prayer, Saul prayed for direction and power to fulfil the great call on his life. In the same way, we also can seek God for direction and empowerment to fulfil his call to vocation, business, ministry, or service in our lives. Three day fasts are not only powerful, but are practical for most people to try.

Twenty-One-Day Fasts

In recent times, the twenty-one-day fast has become popular in churches around the world. It's normally a partial fast, based on the prophet Daniel's deleting meat and rich foods from his diet for three weeks, while he prayed and sought God. Some Christians do a complete fast for three weeks, but for most it's partial. At the end of the fast, an angel appeared to Daniel and said, "I am here to explain what will happen to your people in the future, for this vision concerns a time yet to come." [24] The angel also explained that he had to fight an evil spirit to get to Daniel, which is why it took three weeks.

---

[22]   Acts 9:11
[23]   See Acts 9:17
[24]   Daniel 10:14

The angel not only revealed Israel's future to Daniel, but also the future of world powers, right to the end of the age. When we need revelation of God's will and future for our lives or children, or need breakthrough against satanic powers, a twenty-one-day partial fast may be just the thing to see them happen.

Forty-Day Fasts

Moses fasted for forty days on Mt Sinai when God gave him the Law, thus inaugurating the Old Covenant. Jesus fasted forty days at the beginning of his ministry, to receive power to help him inaugurate the New Covenant of grace. This happened after his water baptism and filling with the Holy Spirit.[25] The Bible records, "Jesus, full of the Holy Spirit...was led by the Spirit in the wilderness, where he was tempted by the devil for forty days. Jesus ate nothing all that time and became very hungry." [26] We may be filled with the Holy Spirit, but sometimes the Spirit will lead us into a wilderness of trial and testing. We haven't done anything wrong; rather the Lord wants to give us greater victory over sin and Satan.

Jesus defeated Satan's temptations and the result was that, "Jesus returned to Galilee, in the power of the Spirit." [27] Numbers of Christians throughout history and today, have fasted and prayed for forty days, to see the same outcome. Some have done a partial fast while others have fasted completely, except perhaps for some juice and broth. This is a serious type of fast.

---

[25] See Luke 3:21-22
[26] Luke 4:1-2
[27] Luke 4:14 (NIV)

Jesus was led by the Spirit into the wilderness for his forty-day fast, and it is best for anyone contemplating such a fast to have a clear leading of the Holy Spirit to do it.

Conclusion

These are some of the Biblical fasts mentioned, but fasting can be any length: one day, two days, three days, ten days and so on. And these can be complete fasts or partial fasts, or any variation that you decide. Greta and I mostly do one to three-day complete fasts, though on occasions we have done longer ones. We have also fasted partially for twenty-one days by skipping our usual breakfast each day to help us have greater sharpness in our morning prayer times. As with prayer, more fasting is better than less fasting; some fasting is better than no fasting.

Whatever duration we decide on, know that the devil will try to point out someone who did a longer fast, suggesting that our smaller efforts are worthless. Realise that our few hours or days of fasting can be just as pleasing to the Father as a much longer fast. It's the heart attitude that he notices, not so much the length of time. If you have never fasted before, start small and let the Holy Spirit grow your capacity. Group prayer and fasting can be a blessing in this regard. We may struggle to do a lengthy fast on our own, but a church can do it far more easily by recruiting members to take a day or more each.

Fasting and prayer will strengthen us to do God's will and allow us to fulfil his destiny for our lives. It will help us to repent of sin and defeat it, and release a greater power of the Holy Spirit through us.

We can be sure that the Father will honour our faltering steps into this realm, and provide grace and strength through his Spirit to do it. And who knows what rewards will come as a result?

Fasting and prayer do indeed form a potent duo. In the next chapter, we will discover one of the most significant areas that they should be used for.

chapter twelve

YOUR PRAYERS CAN HELP SAVE THE LOST

"I urge you, first of all," implores the apostle Paul, "to pray for all people. Ask God to help them; intercede on their behalf, and give thanks for them. Pray this way for kings and all who are in authority so that we can live peaceful and quiet lives marked by godliness and dignity. This is good and pleases God our Saviour, who wants everyone to be saved and to understand the truth." [1]

When an apostle urges us, we should listen. If we want to please God, says Paul, then we must make it a priority to pray especially for two groups. For leaders, so that they will govern society well.[2] And for lost souls, because the Father wants everyone to be saved. In this chapter, we will discover

---

[1]   1 Timothy 2:1-4

[2]   If leaders govern according to the Judeo-Christian principles that have framed society for centuries, nations will enjoy peace and rest. This in turn will allow the Church to more easily evangelise the lost.

what it means to be lost, how serious it is, and how we can pray for lost people to be found.

John Newton Was Lost

John Newton [3] went to sea at age eleven. Later press-ganged into the Royal Navy, he tried to desert and was flogged, receiving ninety-six lashes. Incensed at this brutal punishment, he briefly contemplated murdering the captain and taking his own life by jumping overboard. Eventually he left the navy, and served on ships that transported slaves from Africa to the Americas. Not only did he support the slave trade, he later captained a number of vessels involved in the immoral practice. Gambling, drunkenness, and extreme profanity were his constant companions. John Newton was lost – not geographically, but spiritually.

Jesus spoke of this lost condition at length when he taught the parables of the lost sheep, the lost coin, and the lost son.[4] A shepherd had one hundred sheep, but one went missing, so he left the ninety-nine to search for it. A woman had ten valuable coins, but could find only nine. She turned her house over searching for the lost one, and rejoiced when she found it. A loving father had a younger son who took his inheritance to a far country and squandered it on riotous living. Finally, he returned home ashamed, but his father welcomed him, restored him to full sonship, and celebrated his return. Seeking to assuage the resentment of his older son, the father appealed to him, "Your brother was dead and has come back to life! He was lost, but

---

[3]   John Newton, 1725-1807
[4]   See Luke 15

now he is found!" [5]

In these stories, the shepherd, the woman, and the father represent a loving God who seeks to restore lost humanity to himself. "There is more joy in heaven over one lost sinner who repents and returns to God," Jesus stressed, "than over ninety-nine others who are righteous and haven't strayed away!" [6] God loves lost people and longs for them to be found. Summarising his entire mission to earth, Jesus said, "For the Son of Man came to seek and save those who are lost." [7]

Even debauched John Newton found God's grace. Caught in a severe Atlantic storm that threatened to sink his ship, Newton prayed to God for mercy. Soon after, the storm calmed, and all on board were spared. Newton gave his life to Christ, and later became an Anglican priest. He even campaigned for the abolition of the slave trade.

Newton wrote numerous hymns, but one has especially stood the test of time and remains popular to this day. It captured his life's story, and resonates with every lost soul that has found forgiveness:

> Amazing grace! How sweet the sound.
> That saved a wretch like me.
> I once was lost, but now am found.
> Was blind but now I see.

Today, we still sing, "I once was lost, but now am found," but much of the modern Church doesn't understand how serious being lost is.

The Awful Consequences of Being Lost

Explaining what it is like to be spiritually lost, the apostle Paul wrote:

> You used to live in sin, just like the rest of the world, obeying the devil – the commander of the powers in the unseen world. He is the spirit at work in the hearts of those who refuse to obey God. All of us used to live that way, following the passionate desires and inclinations of our sinful nature. By our very nature we were subject to God's anger, just like everyone else.[8]

As a father, God wants to show mercy to sinners, but as a judge, he is angry at sin and will punish it. And sin's lethal web has caught the entire human race in its strands: "*Everyone* has sinned; *we all* fall short of God's glorious standard."[9] God is so holy that if we break even one of his commandments, it's enough to separate us from him. "But your iniquities have separated you from your God;" says the Bible, "your sins have hidden his face from you, so that he will not hear."[10] If we die in this state of separation, it will force God to say, "I wanted you to live with me for eternity. But now by my justice, I must

[8]   Ephesians 2:2-3
[9]   Romans 3:23, emphasis mine.
[10]   Isaiah 59:2 (NIV)

send you to a place separated from me." And any place where God isn't, is hell.

In a vision, the apostle John saw the ultimate, terrible fate of the lost: "But the cowardly, the unbelieving, the vile, the murderers, the sexually immoral, those who practice magic arts, the idolaters and all liars—they will be consigned to the fiery lake of burning sulphur. This is the second death." [11] In today's Church we have diluted how horrific it is to be lost, for fear of offending people. Yet, without this bad news, there would be no good news. Jesus announced at the beginning of his ministry, "The Spirit of the Lord is upon me, for he has anointed me to bring Good News." [12]

The Good News is Really Good

The good news is that the Father sent Jesus our Messiah into the world to create a pathway back to him. He did this by dying on the cross, taking the judicial punishment for all our sins upon himself. "For Christ also suffered once for sins," wrote the apostle Peter, "the righteous for the unrighteous, to bring you to God. He was put to death in the body but made alive in the Spirit." [13] When, like John Newton, we turn to God, ask forgiveness for our sins, and receive Christ into our lives, something remarkable happens. God wipes the record of our sin clean, and credits to us the perfect righteousness of his son Jesus.

---

[11]   Revelation 21:8 (NIV)
[12]   Luke 4:18a
[13]   1 Peter 3:18 (NIV)

"God made you alive with Christ," explains the apostle Paul, "for he forgave all our sins. He cancelled the record of the charges against us and took it away by nailing it to the cross." [14] God erased from his heavenly record book every sin we committed. Then he wrote our names in the Book of Life. If our names are in that book, God will allow us to enter the new eternal paradise that he will one day create.[15] My book *Afterlife* explains in detail the wonders of the coming new world and what it will be like to live in it.[16]

How to Help the Lost Be Found

As wonderful as this good news is for the saved, it is terrible for the lost. That's why Jesus commanded his followers to tell people everywhere about him. God loves lost people, and there are over 5.5 billion of them on planet earth. Today, the world calls good evil and evil good. Not only is sin tolerated, it is celebrated, and even legislated. This has caused God to remove his protection, and nations are falling prey to climate disasters, civil unrest, wars, racial division, pandemics, corrupt governments and so on.

The Father wants us to be concerned for this lost world. While we can't be responsible for the entire world, we can be for those we are close to: family, extended family, friends, close neighbours and workmates, and so on. Showing them love and kindness, explaining the good news as we have opportunity,

---

[14] Colossians 2:13b-14
[15] See Revelation 21:27
[16] *Afterlife* is available from our website www.spiritlife.org.nz and online bookstores.

and being a channel of supernatural power will help awaken them to God's love. But this is not enough – something more is needed. That something is prayer.

The Bible tells us the reason why: "Satan, who is the god of this world, has blinded the minds of those who don't believe. They are unable to see the glorious light of the Good News. They don't understand this message about the glory of Christ, who is the exact likeness of God." [17] Prayer is the only way to defeat this spiritual blindness. When we pray for lost people, it allows the Holy Spirit to work in their lives to bring them to Christ.

Describing the Holy Spirit's role in this process, Jesus said, "When he comes, he will convict the world of its sin, and of God's righteousness, and of the coming judgment." [18] The Holy Spirit shows people that they are sinners, reveals the righteousness available in Christ, and warns them of a coming day of judgment, when all will answer to God for what they have done. And he is excellent at doing it.

A Surprising Salvation Story

After I graduated from university and completed teachers' training college, I returned to Blenheim to teach mathematics at Marlborough Boys' College, my old high school. At the same time, Jane and I led a church plant in Picton, a picturesque seaside town a half-hour's drive north of Blenheim. Two years later, the church had grown sufficiently for the elders to ask me to lead it fulltime. So I told my classes that I would not

---

[17]   2 Corinthians 4:4
[18]   John 16:8

128

return the following year, as I was going to pastor the Picton Elim Church. Ten years later, I received this letter from one of my former pupils:

Dear Mr Peters,

You may remember me as a pupil of yours at Marlborough Boys' College. I am writing to tell you I am now a Christian. My memory recalls me wondering what gives someone so much courage to stand at the head of a class of rowdy school boys and say that he is leaving to become a pastor of the Elim Church. The Lord never gave me any peace from that day on until nine weeks ago, when I asked him into my life.

I admired you for telling us all, and although I didn't really understand, I knew that what you were doing you felt very strongly about. I did know it was for Jesus Christ. Now I understand totally. I had to tell you of my new life as you were the first of many to tell me about the Lord, even with those few words that day at school. I am getting married in three and a half weeks, and my fiancé asked the Lord into her life the day after I did. I just wanted to tell you that one of your past pupils has become a Christian.

The Lord never gave me any peace from that day on. My few words were a seed that the Holy Spirit then watered through other people. Never underestimate what the Spirit can do with the seeds we plant in others, especially if we pray.

Jesus' Commission to the Church

When Jesus saved the apostle Paul, he commissioned him with this task: "I am sending you to the Gentiles to open their eyes, so they may turn from darkness to light and from the power of Satan to God. Then they will receive forgiveness for their sins and be given a place among God's people, who are set apart by faith in me." [19] Listen to God's heartbeat in these words. Gentiles were non-Jewish people far from him, yet he longed for them to be in his kingdom.

The apostle succeeded in doing what Jesus commanded him to do. Some twenty years later, he wrote, "I have brought the Gentiles to God by my message and by the way I lived before them. I have won them over by the miracles done through me as signs from God – all by the power of God's Spirit. In this way, I have fully presented the Good News of Christ." [20] Paul's strategy to bring people to Christ is timeless. Three things were involved:

First, *proclamation* (telling them the good news).

Second, *demonstration* (showing them the good news by the way we live, and by supernatural signs and wonders).

Third, *intercession* (praying that they will receive the good news). Paul constantly asked churches to pray for him to preach the gospel effectively.[21]

---

[19]   Acts 26: 17b-18
[20]   Romans 15:18-19 (NLT 1996 version)
[21]   See, for example, 2 Thessalonians 3:1: "We ask you to pray for us. Pray that the Lord's message will spread rapidly and be honoured wherever it goes."

Any church that does all three will see lost people saved.

A Challenge

May I encourage you to intercede at least weekly for those in your world who do not yet know the Lord. Use some of the scriptures in this chapter to help you pray. And from time to time, add fasting to your prayers. If we pray persistently for them, it will help open their hearts to the message of the gospel and overcome their spiritual blindness. We will then have the joy of living with them in eternity.

As we pray for the lost people in our immediate world, there will also be times when the Holy Spirit will widen our prayer focus. A news report, concern for a nation or people group, anger at an injustice, a vision or dream – any of these may point us to intercede for a particular country or group. These past five or six years, for example, Greta and I have prayed for spiritual awakening in not only our own nation, but also in the United States and the United Kingdom. The more we have prayed, the more we have felt God's love for these two nations.

Others may have different countries or people groups assigned to them. One time, when praying over a map of the world, the Lord drew my attention to the Arctic Circle. For some months I interceded for the indigenous people who lived there. Then the assignment lifted. Once you start interceding for the lost, the Holy Spirit may surprise you with some unusual short or long-term prayer assignments. And if we persist, the results may amaze us.

The Powerful Effects of Persistent Prayer

The following story illustrates the effects of persistent intercession on lost people. George Müller was a renowned Christian philanthropist and evangelist in Victorian England who cared for over ten thousand orphans through his orphanages in Bristol. He also established schools that educated more than one hundred thousand children.

One time, he became concerned for five of his non-believing friends. So he began to pray for them. After some months, one of them came to the Lord. Ten years later, two others were converted. It took twenty-five years of intercession before the fourth man was saved. Müller persevered in prayer another twenty-seven years for the fifth friend, and throughout those five decades never gave up hope that he would accept Christ. Then Müller died. Soon after the funeral, however, the last friend surrendered his life to Christ.

Here is the point: there are some people in your life who may come to Christ quickly. Others may take years or even decades. And some you may not see saved in your lifetime – but you will see it from heaven. Never give up. Never stop believing, and never stop praying. "The earnest prayer of a righteous person," declares the Bible, "has great power and produces wonderful results." [22] If we pray, it doesn't matter how spiritually dead or lost people appear, God can still reach them. "But God is so rich in mercy, and he loved us so much," says the Bible, "that even though we were dead because of our sins, he gave us life when he raised Christ from the dead." [23]

---

[22]   James 5:16b
[23]   Ephesians 2:4-5

If we persist in prayer, we may literally shape the future of not only individuals, but also nations. "The man or woman who mobilises the Christian church to pray," wrote South African pastor and author Andrew Murray,[24] "will make the greatest contribution to world evangelisation in history."

In the next chapter, we will look at another group of people who desperately need our persistent prayers – the next generation.

---

[24]   Andrew Murray, 1828-1917

chapter thirteen

THE NEXT GENERATION NEEDS OUR PRAYERS

Currently, over half of all people on earth are under the age of thirty. And they are a generation in peril. History tells us that whenever God is about to do something that will radically change the world, Satan's hatred erupts against the young. Before Israel's delivery from captivity in Egypt, Pharaoh tried to kill all male babies born to the Hebrews. But Moses survived and delivered the nation from slavery. At the time of Jesus' birth, King Herod killed all the male children in Bethlehem under the age of two. Jesus survived, however, and delivered the world from slavery to sin and death.

Today, Satan's strategies against the next generation are even worse. First, he has tried to destroy them. In 2021, over 3.5 million people[1] died from Covid-19. In the same year, the World Health Organisation estimates 73 million babies were

---

[1]   See www.worldometers.info/coronavirus/coronavirus-death-toll, accessed 8/02/22

aborted, which is nothing less than a genocide of the unborn.[2] Second, if the devil can't kill them in the womb, he seeks to defile them with sexual immorality, pornography, addictions, and so on. Third, he also wants to distract them with the many false causes that are so popular with the young today. If ever a generation needed our prayers, it is this one.

This current satanic onslaught is because the world is accelerating towards the second coming of Christ. The devil wants to prevent the next generation from becoming what God desires them to be – the greatest end-time army of harvest workers and kingdom influencers the world has ever seen.

A Vision

In 2011, while Greta and I holidayed in Salcombe, England, the Holy Spirit gave me a vision. I saw a brilliant orange sky, unlike anything I had seen naturally. Slowly the orb of the sun rose, and it became too dazzling to look at. Then I saw that it was actually the face of Jesus. Finally, his entire body stood between heaven and earth.[3] His hands were like fire, and from him marched an army of God's people clothed in white.

Fire leapt from Jesus' hands onto each of them, setting them ablaze. As I turned to see where they were going, I saw the globe of a darkened earth. Suddenly, bursts of fire and light exploded in many places around the world. The Lord said to me, "These are my awakened, burning ones who carry my glory into the

---

[2] See www.who.int/news-room/fact- sheets/detail/abortion, accessed 8/02/22

[3] See Malachi 4:2: "But for you who fear my name, the Sun of Righteousness will rise with healing in his wings."

earth. Wherever they go they bring my fire and light. Time is short and I am coming soon. My people must awake from sleep."

Over time, as Greta and I have prayed into this vision, we have become convinced that this army largely represents the under thirty-five generation. That is why Satan is so viciously attacking them – he wants to terminate God's purposes for them. While the older generations will certainly play a part in this great army, our main role will be to encourage the next generation, and to intercede for them. Among them are our children, grandchildren, nephews, nieces, cousins, and others. We must leave a legacy for good in the lives of those younger than us.

Great King, Terrible Legacy

A righteous man, King Hezekiah of Judah helped turn his people back to God.[4] The revival that followed even spilled over into neighbouring Israel, who, two centuries before, had split from Judah to form their own kingdom. When Assyria later invaded the land, Hezekiah and the prophet Isaiah prayed to the Lord, who sent an angel to kill 185 thousand Assyrian soldiers. It was an incredible victory, and brought Hezekiah to the attention of nearby nations, who came to pay him tribute.

After all this, Hezekiah fell terminally ill. While visiting him, Isaiah gave the king a message: "This is what the Lord says: 'Set your affairs in order, for you are going to die. You will not recover from this illness.' " [5] Despite this sombre prophecy, Hezekiah

---

[4]   See 2 Chronicles 29-32
[5]   Isaiah 38:1b

prayed for healing. "Remember, O Lord," he pleaded, "how I have always been faithful to you and have served you single-mindedly, always doing what pleases you." [6]

The Lord relented, and gave him another fifteen years of life. The story of this miracle spread to neighbouring nations and the king of Babylon sent envoys to congratulate Hezekiah. Wanting to impress them, the king showed them all the treasures of his kingdom.

Because of Hezekiah's pride, God sent Isaiah to warn him, "The time is coming when everything in your palace – all the treasures stored up by your ancestors until now – will be carried off to Babylon. Nothing will be left. Some of your very own sons will be taken away into exile." [7] The king's reaction to this prophecy was staggering: " 'This message you have given me from the Lord is good.' For the king was thinking, 'At least there will be peace and security during my lifetime.' " [8]

Three years after being healed, Hezekiah celebrated the birth of his son Manasseh. Twelve years later, Manasseh became king in place of his father. Hezekiah, however, failed to pass his faith onto his son. Manasseh became the most evil king that both Judah and Israel had seen. Hezekiah squandered the extra years given to him, and represents those who are unconcerned for the next generation.

The king began well – he experienced revival, victory over the formidable Assyrian army, miraculous healing, wealth beyond

---

[6]   Isaiah 38:3
[7]   Isaiah 39:6-7
[8]   Isaiah 39:8

measure, and enjoyed the favour of surrounding nations. He had it all. And yet he failed in his greatest task – to leave a righteous legacy. We cannot afford to do the same.

What We Can Do for the Next Generation

Besides being godly examples to the next generation, and equipping and mentoring them to love and serve God, one of the older generation's greatest roles is to pray for them. Our prayers help to create a pathway of destiny for our descendants. If you are a parent, pray for your children. If you are a grandparent, pray for your children and grandchildren. If you don't have children, pray for younger family members and relatives. Intercession for the next generation, both inside and outside the Church, will help them overcome a vicious enemy who wages war on their souls.

During our weekly fasting day, Greta and I prioritise praying together for our children and grandchildren by name. We also include our nephews and nieces. As explained in chapter nine, we use various Bible verses to intercede for them. One of the scriptures that we pray for them is: "I will pour out my Spirit on your offspring, and my blessing on your descendants." [9] This is a powerful promise, and though spoken to Israel, it applies to all God's children. Not a week goes by where we do not pray and declare this over our living descendants, and the ones yet to be born. We want them to have lifelong relationships, and be blessed with good careers, provision, health and so on. But even more, we want the Holy Spirit to empower them to serve

---

[9]   Isaiah 44:3b (NIV)

God in whatever sphere of life he assigns to them.

"For we are God's handiwork," states the Bible, "created in Christ Jesus to do good works, which God prepared in advance for us to do." [10] This is something that Greta and I pray for ourselves – that until the day we die, we will discover the works God has prepared for us to do, and walk in them. And we pray it for our children and grandchildren even more. Whatever state your descendants are in currently, they are God's handiwork. They are not destined for a meaningless existence on earth. God has planned many wonderful things for them to do, that will help bless others and advance his kingdom. In discovering these works, our descendants will live with purpose.

You may have children who do not yet know Jesus as their saviour, or who once did, but now are far from God. Pray for them. Listen to this great promise from God: "The prey will be freed from the mighty warrior and captives will be rescued from a conqueror! For I will fight with those who fight with you, and I myself will save your children." [11] When we pray consistently for our children, God will wrestle them free from the powers of darkness that may have taken them captive, and save them. It may take years, but he will do it.

One of my sons became involved in drugs at high school. For twelve years, he immersed himself in the drug scene. The Holy Spirit led Jane and me to do two things: love him unconditionally and pray for him unceasingly. After Jane passed away, God convicted him and he decided to follow the Lord again. Since then, he has blossomed spiritually and become a leader in his

---

[10]   Ephesians 2:10 (NIV)
[11]   Isaiah 49:25 (TPT)

church. He writes of that time:

> There was a really dark time in my life, where I was living away from God. I was addicted to drugs but deceived and actually enjoyed the life I lived. I was dealing and committing crime, but wasn't fazed. One thing I will never forget from that time is the love and prayers of my parents. They loved me through it all and it made such a difference. I knew I always had somewhere to go, someone to talk to, and an open door.
>
> Looking back now, I am so grateful for that and know it saved my life. Now when I think of my heavenly Father, I feel I can relate more to the unconditional love we live in as sons and daughters of God.

Jude, the brother of Jesus, writes, "Now to him who is able to keep you from falling and to present you without blemish before the presence of his glory with rejoicing." [12] This is a picture of judgment day when, after Jesus returns to earth, believers will stand before him to receive their reward for serving him. The Father wants this to be a day of joy and celebration, not one of dismay. If we pray this scripture for ourselves and our descendants, God will do it. No matter how far they are from God, or how weak their faith may be, he is able. This is true not only of our descendants, but also of the lost generation growing up today.

---

[12]   Jude 24 (RSV)

Other Promises to Pray for the Next Generation

Scattered throughout the Bible are prophetic promises that speak about the next generation. Conditional on the older generation walking with God, they reveal his love for the young. Today, so many young people live without any sense of hope for the future. Jesus wants to recruit them into his army of awakened ones to serve him in these last days. The greatest things we can do for them is to model a sincere love for God and pray for them. The Bible promises great rewards to those who do so. Here are a few of them:

"Blessed are those who fear the Lord, who find great delight in his commands. Their children will be mighty in the land." [13]

"How joyous are those who love the Lord and bow low before God, ready to obey him! Your reward will be prosperity, happiness, and well-being...Your children will bring you joy as they gather around your table. Yes, this is God's generous reward for those who love him." [14]

"Our children will also serve him. Future generations will hear about the wonders of the Lord. His righteous acts will be told to those not yet born. They will hear about everything he has done." [15]

"Whoever fears the Lord has a secure fortress, and for their children it will be a refuge." [16]

---

[13] Psalm 112:1-2 (NIV)
[14] Psalm 128:1-2, 3b-4 (TPT)
[15] Psalm 22:30-31
[16] Proverbs 14:26 (NIV)

A Global Sensation

During the Covid crisis of recent years, a special song achieved phenomenal global success. Composed by Elevation Worship, with the words taken largely from the Bible,[17] it became an anthem in a world reeling from the effects of a pandemic. In various nations, scores of churches joined together to sing it over their countries via video. It has encouraged millions who have listened to it, for it amplifies God's longing for a broken world. It is the song *The Blessing*.[18] Here are some of the lyrics:

> The Lord bless you and keep you.
> Make his face shine upon you.
> And be gracious to you.
> The Lord turn his face toward you
> And give you peace.
>
> May his favour be upon you.
> And a thousand generations.
> And your family and your children.
> And their children, and their children.

I am sure that part of its appeal has been the declaration of blessing over multiple generations. When I sing that part of the song, faith surges within me for our descendants. It is the highest privilege to pray for and declare blessing over the next generation.

---

[17]   See Numbers 6:22-26
[18]   Elevation Worship, "The Blessing", © 2020, from the album *Graves into Gardens*.

A Poem

Amy Carmichael [19] was an Irish missionary to India, who had a passion to rescue Hindu temple children. Temple children were mainly young girls dedicated to the gods, then usually forced into prostitution to earn money for the priests. Families often sold unwanted children to the temples, if they needed extra money. Amy gave herself to the next generation, praying for them and freeing many from their appalling fate. She wrote the following poem, and it is perhaps a fitting finale for this chapter and an intercessory cry for all who are concerned for the next generation:

> Father, hear us, we are praying.
> Hear the words our hearts are saying.
> We are praying for our children.
>
> Keep them from the powers of evil,
> From the secret, hidden peril.
> Father, hear us for our children.
>
> From the worldling's hollow gladness,
> From the sting of faithless sadness,
> Father, Father, keep our children.
>
> Through life's troubled waters steer them.
> Through life's bitter battles cheer them.
> Father, Father, be thou near them.
> And wherever they may bide,
> Lead them home at eventide.

---

[19]   Amy Carmichael, 1867-1951

chapter fourteen

HOW TO DEAL WITH UNANSWERED PRAYER

From a human perspective, it appears that some prayers go unanswered. From a divine perspective, all prayers are answered. As one pastor put it, "God answers prayer with go, slow, grow, or no."

Go – the answer comes quickly.

Slow – the answer takes time to come, to teach us persistence, and to allow for God's precision timing.

Grow – the answer is delayed because God wants to grow our character to be able to handle the answer when it comes.

No – a loving Father knows that what we asked for would harm us, it wasn't his will, or he has better plans for us.

In this chapter, we will discover some of the obstacles to prayer, so that by avoiding them, we can see our requests answered.

Vague Prayers

God answers specific prayers more readily than vague prayers. When we are learning to pray, he may answer general prayers to encourage us. But as we mature, he wants us to hear his voice and pray specifically. Jesus taught us to pray, "Your will be done on earth as it is in heaven."[1] Knowing his will – both from scripture and prophetic revelation – will help us pray more effectively.

When South Korean pastor David Cho[2] began his ministry shortly after the Korean war, he was single and destitute. Living in a small rented room, he had no desk, chair, or bed. He ate, slept, and studied on the floor. Each day he walked long distances to win lost souls. Tiring of his conditions and feeling that a child of God should have the tools to do his work, Cho prayed for a desk, a chair, and a bicycle.

Months passed with no answer. One day, feeling depressed, he complained to God about the delay. At that moment, the Holy Spirit spoke to him:

---

[1]   Luke 11:2b (NKJV)
[2]   David Yonggi Cho, 1936-2021

You beg me, demanding every kind of request but ask in vague terms. Don't you know that there are dozens of kinds of desks, chairs and bicycles? You simply asked for a desk, a chair and a bicycle. You did not ask for a specific desk, a specific chair and a specific bicycle.

Cho prayed again, and this time was far more specific:

> I gave the Lord the size of the desk and that it was to be made of Philippine mahogany. I wanted the best kind of chair, one made with an iron frame with rollers on the tips so that when I sat on it I could push myself around. I wanted to have a strong sturdy bicycle, and at that time bicycles made in the United States were the best. So I said, "Father, I want to have a bicycle made in the United States with gears on the side so that I can even regulate the speed."

> I continued to praise the Lord every day for the things I had asked for and sure enough when God's time came, I had every one of those things. Until this experience I had always prayed in vague terms, but from that time I never prayed in vague terms any more. [3]

Now someone may say, "Doesn't God know best anyway? So why not let him choose?" There are definitely occasions when we don't know what the specifics should be, and so we can leave them to the Lord.

---

[3]   Abridged from www.davidcho.com/neweng/bc6-1.asp, accessed 28/09/21

However, Father wants us to become mature sons and daughters who grow in faith. Specific prayers require greater faith.

After the Lord healed me of the grief of Jane's death, I wanted to marry again. So I began to pray that I would meet someone. Around that time, I read in the book of Genesis the story of Jacob meeting his future wife Rachel. The Bible's description of her captivated me: "Rachel was beautiful in every way, with a lovely face and shapely figure." [4] *I would like my next wife to be exactly like that* I thought to myself. So I prayed, "I'd like to have a Rachel please, Lord!" God certainly delivered when I met Greta, and I regularly thank him for bringing us together.

Unconfessed Sin

If there is known sin in our lives that we refuse to repent of, it will block prayer being answered. Such sin gives the devil a foothold to oppress us and hinder prayer. Now God is not waiting for us to be perfect before he will answer prayer. "The Lord is like a father to his children," says the Bible, "tender and compassionate to those who fear him. For he knows how weak we are; he remembers we are only dust." [5] Sin that we keep stumbling in, but want victory over, will not block our prayers. Rather, it is wilful sin that we know is wrong and refuse to forsake that will do that.

"We know that God doesn't listen to sinners," records the Bible, "but he is ready to hear those who worship him and do

---

[4]   Genesis 29:17 (NLT 1996 version)
[5]   Psalm 103:13-14

his will." [6] The psalmist wrote, "If I had cherished sin in my heart, the Lord would not have listened." [7]

Another tactic of Satan is to tempt husbands and wives to sin by dishonouring one another in marriage. "You husbands must give honour to your wives," instructed the apostle Peter. "Treat your wife with understanding as you live together. She may be weaker [8] than you are, but she is your equal partner in God's gift of new life. Treat her as you should so your prayers will not be hindered." [9] This appeal came straight after Peter had urged wives to respect their husbands. [10] Honouring one another in marriage will add potency to our prayer lives.

Although deliberate sin blocks God's ears to our prayers, there is one prayer that he will always answer. It is the prayer of confession. The Bible says, "If we confess our sins to him, he is faithful and just to forgive us our sins and to cleanse us from all wickedness." [11] Speaking about Jesus, the writer to the Hebrews says, "For we have not a high priest who is unable to sympathise with our weaknesses, but one who in every respect has been tempted as we are, yet without sin. Let us then with confidence draw near to the throne of grace, that we may receive mercy and find grace to help in time of need." [12]

---

[6] John 9:31
[7] Psalm 66:18 (NIV)
[8] Peter is not suggesting that women are weaker mentally, emotionally, or spiritually. The majority of ancient women were disadvantaged economically, legally, and politically. They had less power and fewer rights in society than men. Peter wanted husbands to be considerate of the more vulnerable situation of their wives and not exploit them.
[9] 1 Peter 3:7
[10] See 1 Peter 3:5-6
[11] 1 John 1:9
[12] Hebrews 4:15-16 (RSV)

Wrong Motives

"You don't have what you want because you don't ask God for it." says the apostle James. "And even when you ask, you don't get it because your motives are all wrong – you want only what will give you pleasure." [13] One obvious reason prayers are not answered is because we don't ask. We think that our own efforts will be enough without God's help. Often prayer is a last resort when it should be the first resort.

And if we pray with wrong motives, God will not answer. Selfishness and self-indulgence may tempt us, and can influence our praying. We don't need perfect motives for God to answer our prayers, just soft hearts, so that he can correct us. A non-answer may be a sign to ask the Holy Spirit to show us if we are praying incorrectly. When our praying aligns with what he wants, amazing things happen.

When young Solomon, King David's son, became king of Israel, he felt overwhelmed with the task and prayed, "Give me an understanding heart so that I can govern your people well and know the difference between right and wrong. For who by himself is able to govern this great people of yours?" [14] God was so pleased that he had asked with such a pure motive that he said to him:

> Because you have asked for wisdom in governing my people with justice and have not asked for a long life or wealth or the death of your enemies – I will give you what you asked for!

---

[13]   James 4:2b-3
[14]   1 Kings 3:9

I will give you a wise and understanding heart such as no one else has had or ever will have! And I will also give you what you did not ask for – riches and fame! No other king in all the world will be compared to you for the rest of your life! [15]

Prayer with the right intentions brings great pleasure to God and he will not only answer our requests but give us more besides.

Timing

Some years ago, I asked the Lord for a theme for the coming year. In my Bible reading that day, I read, "Do not be impatient for the Lord to act; travel steadily along his path." [16] The Holy Spirit highlighted the word *steadily* and I knew that this was the message for the year ahead. The next day, a prophet rang to share a verse he felt was for me: "The Lord you are seeking will suddenly come to his Temple." [17] My friend said that the word *suddenly* was emphasised to him. I thanked him, finished the call, and said to the Lord, "These are opposites. One of us is wrong. Who is it?"

The Lord replied, "Both are correct. Too many of my people want my suddenlies, without being willing to walk steadily. If they will walk steadily, and seek me, there will be suddenlies." We want the suddenly without the steadily. We want our prayers answered yesterday, but God may not answer for years.

---

[15]   1 Kings 3:11-13
[16]   Psalm 37:34a (NLT 1996 version)
[17]   Malachi 3:1

There are a number of reasons for this. First, he may want to teach us persistence in prayer so that our faith will grow. Second, he is the God of precision timing and will take time to get everything and everyone into the right place for the answer to come. He won't rush this.

Third, and most importantly, perseverance grows our character. "We can rejoice, too, when we run into problems and trials," explains the Bible, "for we know that they help us develop endurance. And endurance develops strength of character." [18] Suddenlies that come without steadilies can be lost because we don't have the character to handle the answer or the inevitable kickback from Satan when a breakthrough comes. The prodigal son received his inheritance too soon, and lost it all.

A few years ago, while in England, I read the following headline in one of the daily newspapers: "Man Who Blew a Lottery Fortune Dies Penniless." The article went on to say, "A £9 million lottery winner who blew his money on drinking, racehorses, and football has died penniless after suffering a heart attack brought on by financial worries." The man lost his marriage, lost his fortune, and died an alcoholic. It made me grateful that our heavenly Father protects us from such ruin by not answering some prayers until we can handle the answer well.

---

[18]   Romans 5:3-4a

Demonic Opposition

Satan hates and fears a praying Christian. There will be times when his demonic forces may attack us with discouragement and weariness, so that we will stop praying. Jesus warned the apostle Peter of an impending spiritual attack when he said, "Simon, Simon, Satan has asked to sift all of you as wheat. But I have prayed for you, Simon, that your faith may not fail. And when you have turned back, strengthen your brothers." [19] Though Peter denied the Lord three times, he did turn back and became a great leader in the early Church.

Satan's goal in spiritual warfare is that our faith will fail. God's goal is that our faith will increase. Here is the key: "Submit yourselves therefore to God. Resist the devil, and he will flee from you. Draw near to God, and he will draw near to you." [20] It is not by accident that these verses are next to each other. Closeness to God is the best form of spiritual warfare and will keep our focus on him, rather than the devil. In the next chapter, we will explore in more detail the spiritual weapons that God has given us to be victorious.

---

[19]   Luke 22:31- 32 (NIV)
[20]   James 4:7-8a (RSV)

Conclusion

To summarise, the key to answered prayer is to pray in agreement with God's will. "And this is the confidence which we have in him," wrote the apostle John, "that if we ask anything according to his will he hears us. And if we know that he hears us in whatever we ask, we know that we have obtained the requests made of him." [21]

To pray God's will means to surrender our lives and the outcome of our prayers to him. Our Father knows what is best for us. And when his best collides with our preference, we need to yield to his will. Jesus prayed that he would not have to endure the agony of the cross: "Father, if you are willing, please take this cup of suffering away from me." But then he added, "Yet I want your will to be done, not mine." [22]

May that be our prayer as well.

---

[21]   1 John 5:14-15 (RSV)
[22]   Luke 22:42

chapter fifteen

PRAYER AND SPIRITUAL WARFARE

For three weeks Daniel prayed and fasted, then an angel brought him God's answer. What the angel said to Daniel was enlightening in more ways than one:

> Don't be afraid, Daniel. Since the first day you began to pray for understanding and to humble yourself before your God, your request has been heard in heaven. I have come in answer to your prayer. But for twenty-one days *the spirit prince of the kingdom of Persia blocked my way.* Then Michael, one of the archangels, came to help me, and I left him there with the spirit prince of the kingdom of Persia. Now I am here to explain what will happen to your people in the future, for this vision concerns a time yet to come.[1]

---

[1]   Daniel 10:12-14, emphasis mine.

The angel revealed Israel's distant future to Daniel in remarkable detail. He also explained that while Daniel prayed, an intense battle had unfolded in the unseen spiritual realm. One of Satan's evil angels, the principality assigned to Persia,[2] had tried to prevent the angel delivering God's answer to Daniel. Finally, through Daniel's persistent prayer and the archangel Michael's help, the answer came.

God had actually answered Daniel's prayer on the first day, but it took three weeks to arrive. At times, evil forces of darkness will oppose our prayers. Persistence in prayer is essential to overcome this. Spiritual warfare and prayer are linked. Most of my prayer times are spent conversing with God. But sometimes direct resistance against the devil's works is necessary. Usually, the Holy Spirit will help us sense when we are dealing with satanic opposition, so that we pray accordingly.

Spiritual Warfare is Real

"For we are not fighting against flesh-and-blood enemies," explains the Bible, "but against evil rulers and authorities of the unseen world, against mighty powers in this dark world, and against evil spirits in the heavenly places."[3] When the archangel Lucifer and one third of the angels rebelled against God, they were cast out of heaven to earth.[4]

---

[2]   Persia was the dominant world power at the time, and Daniel was an official in its government.

[3]   Ephesians 6:12

[4]   See Revelation 12:7-9 (some scholars see this as not a past event but a future one, albeit reflecting the original casting out of heaven). See also Isaiah 14:4-17 and Ezekiel 28:12-17.

Lucifer became Satan, and the fallen angels became evil spiritual powers under the devil's command.[5]

When Satan later lured Adam and Eve to sin, they unwittingly handed rulership of planet earth to him. Scripture confirms this: "The devil led [Jesus] up to a high place and showed him in an instant all the kingdoms of the world. And he said to him, 'I will give you all their authority and splendour; *it has been given to me*, and I can give it to anyone I want to. If you worship me, it will all be yours.' " [6] Jesus didn't dispute Satan's claim to be ruler of the earth, because at that time it was true.

When Jesus died on the cross to atone for humanity's sin however, Satan lost his right to rule. "He disarmed the spiritual rulers and authorities," writes the apostle Paul. "He shamed them publicly by his victory over them on the cross." [7] Jesus triumphed over sin, death, and Satan by his death and resurrection. He then delegated to his Church the authority to defeat the powers of darkness and set their human captives free.

Respected American pastor Jack Hayford writes, "The New Testament reveals an invisible hierarchy of evil powers who deceive and manipulate human behaviour, thereby advancing satanic strategies. All who are in Christ are placed in authority above these powers, an authority that only spiritual warfare can assert." [8]

---

[5]   There is some debate as to whether demonic spirits are a lower class of fallen angel, or they are the spirits of the giants that resulted from the intermarriage of angels and women, as described in Genesis 6:1-4.

[6]   Luke 4:5-7 (NIV), emphasis mine.

[7]   Colossians 2:15

[8]   Adapted from *Spirit Filled Life Bible*, © 1991 Thomas Nelson, footnote, p. 1788.

When Japan surrendered to the victorious Allies at the end of World War Two, Japanese military forces were still scattered throughout the Pacific. Though the Allies tried to convince them of the surrender, many soldiers did not believe it and kept fighting for months and even years. One officer, Lieutenant Hiroo Onoda, finally surrendered in 1974. He had held out in the Philippine jungle for 29 years after the war ended!

Like the triumphant Allies, we do not fight to attain a victory; rather, we fight to enforce a victory already won. In this battle, we must realise that the devil is not an anti-god. He is a fallen angel, and does not have the same powers as God. The war is not between Satan and God; there is no contest there. Rather the war is between Satan and humankind. And in this conflict, God has given us very powerful weapons to overcome our enemy.

Spiritual Missiles

Today, missiles are the most potent weapons in the military arsenals of most nations. A missile comprises two parts:

First, *a warhead* which carries the explosive that will destroy the target.

Second, *a rocket* to propel the warhead to its target.

The rocket without the warhead is ineffective. It might impress with its trail of fire and smoke, but it will not damage the target in the slightest. And a warhead without a rocket is unusable. Both must be employed together. God has given to every believer a spiritual missile system that is both defensive and offensive. He has given us spiritual warheads and spiritual rockets. In the rest of this chapter, we will discover what these warheads are.

Warheads represent authority. Without authority, our warfare will be in vain. "Look," said Jesus, "I have given you authority over all the power of the enemy, and you can walk among snakes and scorpions and crush them. Nothing will injure you." [9] Snakes and scorpions symbolise evil spiritual powers and demons. If we are under God's authority, then we will have the authority to conquer these evil forces. "So submit to [the authority of] God," says the Bible. "Resist the devil [stand firm against him] and he will flee from you." [10]

There are three powerful warheads of authority that the Father has given to every believer in Jesus.

The Blood of Jesus

The Bible contains many references to the blood of Christ and the last one is revealing: "For the accuser of our brothers and sisters has been thrown down to earth – the one who accuses them before our God day and night. And they have defeated him by the blood of the Lamb and by their testimony. And they did not love their lives so much that they were afraid to die." [11]

Three things allow us to overcome Satan and his accusations. First, the blood of Christ. Second, our confession that Jesus is

---

[9]   Luke 10:19
[10]   James 4:7 (AMP)
[11]   Revelation 12:10b-11

Lord and that we belong to him.[12] Third, refusing to cling to our own lives, even when faced with death.[13] While these last two speak of our commitment to Jesus, the first refers to our standing before God. As a righteous judge, God must punish sin. But Jesus stepped in and took the punishment for us when he shed his blood on the cross.

"For you know that God paid a ransom to save you from the empty life you inherited from your ancestors," writes the apostle Peter. "And it was not paid with mere gold or silver, which lose their value. It was the precious blood of Christ, the sinless, spotless Lamb of God."[14] The apostle Paul put it this way: "[God] is so rich in kindness and grace that he purchased our freedom with the blood of his son and forgave our sins."[15] The whole basis of our acceptance by God rests on the blood of Christ. This is where our authority comes from.

In the previous chapter, we discussed various obstacles to answered prayer. To that list we should add accusation. The devil will assault our character and identity, and highlight our faults, sins, and weaknesses. He will try to cripple us with guilt, shame, and regret over our past. Satan will especially do this when we pray. He will suggest that God won't hear our prayers because of these things. We defeat his relentless accusations by believing and declaring that the blood of Christ has washed

---

[12]   See Romans 10:9: "If you openly declare that Jesus is Lord and believe in your heart that God raised him from the dead, you will be saved."

[13]   See Mark 8:35-36: "If you try to hang on to your life, you will lose it. But if you give up your life for my sake and for the sake of the Good News, you will save it. And what do you benefit if you gain the whole world but lose your own soul?"

[14]   1 Peter 1:18-19

[15]   Ephesians 1:7

away our record of sin and shame. "Because of Christ and our faith in him," declares the Bible, "*we can come fearlessly into God's presence,* assured of his glad welcome." [16]

This powerful warhead alone gives us all the authority we need. But God has generously given us another two.

The Name of Jesus

Speaking of Jesus, the apostle Paul wrote:

> He humbled himself in obedience to God and died a criminal's death on a cross. Therefore, God elevated him to the place of highest honour and gave him the name above all other names, that at the name of Jesus every knee should bow, in heaven and on earth and under the earth, and every tongue declare that Jesus Christ is Lord, to the glory of God the Father. [17]

Jesus is the highest name of all because he has the highest position of all. The readers of Paul's day would have immediately understood the authority that Jesus' name carried. In Roman times, conquered territories were ruled by Roman governors who were under the authority of Caesar and the Roman senate.

Occasionally, Caesar would send an envoy to investigate how the colony was doing, or to carry a command from Rome. On arriving, the envoy would declare, "I come in the name of

---

[16] Ephesians 3:12 (NLT, 1996 version), emphasis mine.
[17] Philippians 2:8-12

Caesar." This announcement meant that the might of the Roman government stood behind the speaker. It was as if Caesar was there in person. The colonial governors were quick to obey whatever the envoy demanded.

In the same way, heaven is the seat of God's government, and earth is a colony that is meant to reflect heaven's values and will. The Church is heaven's envoy, sent into the nations to bring heaven to earth. And we do it in the name of Jesus, the highest name in all the universe. All authority and power is in the name of Jesus. We are to pray in the name of Jesus. We are to heal the sick and cast out demons in the name of Jesus. We are to do good in the name of Jesus. We are to preach the gospel in the name of Jesus.

The phrase *in the name of Jesus* is more than a mere religious formula. It is a declaration that we represent him, and have been given authority by him. By praying in the name of Jesus, we appeal to an authority far greater than ours. "You can ask for anything in my name," promised Jesus, "and I will do it, so that the Son can bring glory to the Father. Yes, ask me for anything in my name, and I will do it!" [18]

The Word of God

The final warhead is the word of God. During Jesus' time in the wilderness, he resisted Satan's temptations by using scripture: "The tempter came to him, and said, 'If you are the Son of God, tell these stones to become bread.' Jesus answered,

---

[18]   John 14:13-14

'It is written: Man shall not live on bread alone, but on every word that comes from the mouth of God.' " [19]

It is written. Quoting God's word releases an authority beyond our own words, and is a powerful weapon. "For the word of God is alive and powerful," declares the Bible. "It is sharper than the sharpest two-edged sword." [20] This alludes to the Roman sword, which unlike most swords of the day, was shorter and had both edges sharpened. It was one of the most formidable close-quarter combat weapons of its time. God's word becomes our sword when we take it from the pages of the Bible and we speak it, especially in prayer and declaration.[21]

Because Christ defeated him, Satan has no power over us. But he can influence us if we believe his lies. Truth defeats lies, and the word of God is the truth. When advising his young co-worker Timothy, the apostle Paul said, "This charge I commit to you, son Timothy, according to the prophecies previously made concerning you, that by them you may wage the good warfare." [22] If personal prophetic words help us win battles, then how much more will scripture.

In this chapter, we have discovered that God has given us three potent warheads of authority: the blood of Christ, the name of Jesus, and the word of God. In the next chapter, we will discover the five spiritual rockets that we can use to deploy these warheads.

---

[19]   Matthew 4:3-4(NIV)
[20]   Hebrews 4:12
[21]   See chapters 8 and 9 for more detail.
[22]   1 Timothy 1:18 (NKJV)

chapter sixteen

THE WEAPONS OF OUR WARFARE

In the previous chapter, we saw that there are times when satanic powers will oppose answers to prayer, or try to afflict us. To help us overcome this opposition, God has given us a spiritual missile system.

These missiles comprise both warheads and rockets. There are three warheads of authority: the blood of Christ, the name of Jesus, and the word of God. In this chapter, we will discover the five rockets that enable us to launch the warheads and exercise that authority.

1. Prayer

After listing the extensive spiritual armour God has given to every Christian,[1] the apostle Paul concludes, "Pray in the Spirit at all times and on every occasion. Stay alert and be persistent in your prayers for all believers everywhere."[2] This type of prayer is a heavy weapon, one of the biggest rockets in our arsenal.

The devil fears a praying Christian or a praying church. This is because prayer in the spiritual realm affects events in the natural realm, as the following story illustrates. The Amalekites were blood relatives of the Israelites,[3] but hated them bitterly. As Israel journeyed from Egypt to the land of Canaan, Amalek attacked. Moses ordered Joshua to lead the Israelite army, while he, his brother Aaron, and brother-in-law Hur [4] climbed a hill that overlooked the battlefield.

On the hilltop, Moses did something unusual – he raised his shepherd's staff into the air. "As long as Moses held up the staff in his hand," records the Bible, "the Israelites had the advantage. But whenever he dropped his hand, the Amalekites gained the advantage."[5] Moses' staff signified divine rescue; lifting his hands signified prayer.[6] The lifting of the staff in Moses' hands, therefore, depicts intercession for divine deliverance.

---

[1] See Ephesians 6:13-18. This armour was based on the components of a Roman soldier's battledress and equipment and each has spiritual significance: the belt of truth, breastplate of righteousness, shoes of peace, shield of faith, helmet of salvation, sword of the Spirit, and prayer.

[2] Ephesians 6:18

[3] Amalek was a grandson of Esau, the brother of Jacob, from whom the nation of Israel descended. Over time, Amalek's descendants became one of Israel's fiercest enemies.

[4] Jewish tradition says that Hur was married to Miriam, Moses' sister.

[5] Exodus 17:11

[6] A shepherd's staff was used to rescue troubled sheep. With his staff, Moses had rescued the Israelites by opposing Pharaoh, parting the Red Sea, and making water spring from a rock. The lifting of hands in the Bible represents prayer (see 1 Timothy 2:8, Psalm 141:2, Lamentations 2:19).

The Bible describes what happened next:

> Moses' arms soon became so tired he could no longer hold them up. So Aaron and Hur found a stone for him to sit on. Then they stood on each side of Moses, holding up his hands. So his hands held steady until sunset. As a result, Joshua overwhelmed the army of Amalek in battle.[7]

At times, the prevailing evil in society may weary our soul, and tempt us to give up. In spite of this, never stop praying. Let's not lower the staff of prayer for ourselves, our family, our nation, and the world. If some battles are too large to fight on our own, seek the help of other praying believers. A united church can prevail and see remarkable victories through prayer. Note that it was Moses' prayer and the army's battlefield skill that brought the victory. It is both prayer and practical mission that transforms people and circumstances on earth.

2. Praise

The Bible says that God is enthroned in the praises of his people.[8] To praise means to honour, glorify, commend, and extol the attributes of someone or something.[9] When we praise God in word or song, it enthrones him over our lives, displacing the powers of darkness that may affect us. The psalmist writes of God's people:

---

[7] Exodus 17:12-13
[8] See Psalm 22:3 (NKJV)
[9] *The Concise Oxford Dictionary*, © 1982, Oxford University Press, Oxford.

God's high and holy praises fill their mouths, for their shouted praises are their weapons of war! These warring weapons will bring vengeance on the nations and every resistant power — to bind kings with chains and rulers with iron shackles. Praise-filled warriors will enforce the judgment decreed against their enemies.[10]

Praise, especially when sacrificial, not only blesses the Lord we love, but also shakes the spiritual realm. When the apostle Paul and the prophet Silas [11] preached the gospel in the city of Philippi, the authorities arrested them, beat them severely, and threw them into prison. Satanic powers had stirred up the city because Paul had confronted a demonic spirit and cast it out of a slave girl.[12]

Yet in the face of this fierce opposition, they did something remarkable: "Around midnight Paul and Silas were praying and singing hymns to God, and the other prisoners were listening. Suddenly, there was a massive earthquake, and the prison was shaken to its foundations. All the doors immediately flew open, and the chains of every prisoner fell off!" [13]

Beaten and bruised, their feet in stocks, Paul and Silas prayed and praised God anyway. Sacrificial praise gets heaven's attention. God will bend his ears to the sound of his children praising him despite their circumstances.

---

[10] Psalm 149:6-9a (TPT)
[11] See Acts 15:22, 32. Silas was a prophet sent from Jerusalem to help Paul.
[12] See Acts 16:16-20
[13] Acts 16:25-26

Suddenlies often come at the midnight hour after we have exhausted all hope of a breakthrough. If we keep praising God, freedom will come. Note that Paul and Silas praised God *in* the prison, not *for* the prison.

Over the sixteen years that I was fulltime caregiver for my first wife Jane, life was not easy for us. Multiple sclerosis trapped her in a prison and trapped me with her. Many times we felt low, but we chose to declare, "Why be downcast O my soul? Put your hope in God, for I will yet praise him. He will put a new song in my mouth, a hymn of praise to our God. Many will see and fear the Lord and put their trust in him." [14] God promoted Jane to heaven where she now praises him face to face. He freed me to travel with Greta and help others trust his goodness despite the circumstances they may face.

Praise, along with worship and prayer, is a powerful weapon that will overcome evil powers. The outward circumstances may not change immediately, but we will be free on the inside. And we don't do it to obtain freedom and victory – we do it because our God is worthy.

3. Preaching

"We are human, but we don't wage war as humans do," writes the apostle Paul. "We use God's mighty weapons, not worldly weapons, to knock down the strongholds of human reasoning and to destroy false arguments. We destroy every proud obstacle that keeps people from knowing God. We capture

---

[14]   Abridged and paraphrased from Psalm 42:5 and Psalm 40:3.

their rebellious thoughts and teach them to obey Christ." [15]

Preaching is one such weapon. When it contains the word of God, is soaked in prayer,[16] and delivered in the anointing of the Holy Spirit, it will break oppression and change wrong mind-sets. If truth is preached consistently over years, not only will it transform lives, but the spiritual atmosphere of a place can also change. Demonic powers, tormented by the truth, will actually leave an area.[17]

Much modern preaching, however, has been reduced to inspirational thoughts and stories, with a light sprinkling of scripture, or none at all. While such messages are pleasant to listen to, they seldom transform their hearers. To preach without the word of God is to fire a rocket without a warhead. Today, there is an urgent need for preaching to become biblically rich. It is God's word that carries the authority to change a life.

Preaching should include inspiring stories and illustrations, but also a generous amount of scripture. If done in love, such preaching will be powerful, convicting, and blessed by the Holy Spirit.[18]

---

[15] 2 Corinthians 10:3-5
[16] Our preaching in public will only be as powerful as our praying in private.
[17] See Luke 4:32-34 where Jesus' teaching caused a demon to beg him to go away. The demon could not stand the authoritative preaching of the truth.
[18] See 1 Thessalonians 1:5 (RSV): "Our gospel came to you not only in word, but also in power and in the Holy Spirit and with full conviction."

4. Binding and Loosing

Binding and loosing may sound strange, but it is a powerful rocket. "I will give you the keys of the kingdom of heaven," Jesus promised. "Whatever you bind on earth will be bound in heaven, and whatever you loose on earth will be loosed in heaven." [19] These keys represent authority and are given to those who believe that Jesus is the son of God and saviour of the world. Keys open and lock doors. *To bind* means to forbid or lock. *To loose* means to permit or unlock.

In the original Greek translation of Jesus' words, the phrase actually says, "whatever you bind on earth shall be, having been bound in heaven and whatever you loose on earth, shall be, having been loosed in heaven." This means that we are to discern what heaven is doing, align with it, and enforce it through binding and loosing. While this may at times involve using the terms "I bind…, I loose…" in prayer, it is far broader than that. For example, preaching of the gospel can loose a person from sin, or casting out a demon will bind its effect in a person's life.

Sometimes, we bind or loose something when we move in the opposite spirit. When flying into a large Asian city some years ago, I had a vision of a beautiful young woman, elegantly dressed, and dripping with jewels. On asking the Lord about it, he said, "It is the satanic power over the city. It is the spirit of seduction to pride and materialism." Knowing that the Lord

---

[19]   Matthew 16:19 (NIV)

also appoints angels to oversee cities,[20] I asked him what he had put over the city.

Immediately, I saw in my mind a very tall angel, clothed in white, with a golden sash around his chest. In his hands, he held many gold bars. "This is my spirit of extravagant generosity. Whenever my people operate in great generosity, they overcome the spirit of seduction to greed and materialism." Greta and I later discovered that many of the inhabitants of that city were very image and material-world conscious, but that the Christians we met were extremely generous.

Whether it is practical action, moving in the opposite spirit, or using the phrases in prayer, binding and loosing are powerful keys to unlock heaven's will on earth.

5. Confession

"Fight the good fight of faith," says the Bible, "lay hold on eternal life, to which you were also called and have confessed the good confession in the presence of many witnesses."[21] The good confession is that Jesus is Lord, and the Christ[22] sent from God. When we confess that, and when we confess his word, it forces satanic powers to cower.

---

[20] See Deuteronomy 32:8, 2 Kings 6:15-17, and Revelation 1:20. These references show that God appoints angels over churches, cities, and nations. Also, there are more angelic powers than satanic powers.

[21] 1 Timothy 6:12(NKJV)

[22] *Christ* means the Anointed One, the promised Messiah who would save the world, restore it to paradise, and restore humankind back to God.

One Bible commentator says, "Our confession of Jesus Christ as Lord invites, and receives, his presence and power over all evil whenever we face it." [23]

It is not just any confession that accomplishes this, but that which agrees with God's word. The Greek word for "confession" in the verse above, comes from the word *homologeo* which means "to say the same thing as another". When we say the same thing about Jesus as Father God says, it saves us. When we say the same thing as the Lord says in scripture, or by prophetic revelation, it will overcome the enemy.

If we are depressed, God's word says the joy of the Lord is our strength. If we are weary, his word says he will give us rest. If we are sick, his word says he is the Lord who heals us. "Death and life," says the Bible, "are in the power of the tongue." [24] The right confession always brings life into any situation. Confession is the same as declaration, and in chapter eight, we saw how it can be a potent component of prayer.

Conclusion

Notice the common point about these five rockets: apart from some aspects of binding and loosing, they all are launched through the mouth. In addition, they are only effective as weapons if the warheads are attached: prayer in the name of Jesus, confession or preaching using the word of God, and so on. Note too that fasting, while not being a weapon, greatly boosts the effectiveness of the weapons above. It is like putting

---

[23]   Roy Hicks, *Spirit Filled Life Bible*, © 1991, Thomas Nelson, p. 1804
[24]   Proverbs 18:21a (NKJV)

super rocket fuel in the missiles.

In spiritual warfare, we are to be neither devil focused, nor fearful. We are to be God focused and have more confidence in Father's ability to bless and protect us than the devil's ability to harm us. "But the Lord is faithful," promises the Bible, "he will strengthen you and guard you from the evil one." [25]

In Greta's and my Call to Arms seminar,[26] which teaches these concepts of prayer and warfare, we often include the song *Break Every Chain*.[27] The chorus says, "There is power in the name of Jesus to break every chain." We explain that by singing it we are using one warhead (the name of Jesus) and two rockets (confession and praise). Many times, God's power has set people free from demonic oppression or sickness as we have sung it. As we use our spiritual rockets and warheads, we will see the Lord do the same for us and those we pray for.

---

[25]   2 Thessalonians 3:3
[26]   See www.spiritlife.org.nz/ministry
[27]   Jesus Culture, "Break Every Chain," © 2009, from the album *Awakening*.

chapter seventeen

FINAL WORDS

"The ministry of preaching is open to few," wrote Leonard Ravenhill. "The ministry of prayer – the highest of all human offices – is open to all." True, the ministry of prayer is open to all, but we have to step into it. It is my hope that this book has inspired you to take that step, or to journey further if you were already on the way. It is also my hope that, if you are a pastor or leader, you will teach the principles in these pages to the people that you lead.

In this book, we have discovered the following truths:

The Lord's Prayer is not so much a prayer to recite, but more a pattern to follow.

The first part of the Lord's Prayer is all about what God wants – that his name be honoured and his kingdom be manifest on earth. The second part is all about us – that our needs for provision, purity, and protection be met.

The Holy Spirit is calling us to make the first part of the Lord's prayer a priority, as much of the Church has camped in the second part. We have reduced prayer to a means of having our needs met.

While there are three types of prayer, it is intercession that opens heaven and transforms earth. All believers are called to intercede.

God has given us other tools such as scripture, declaration, prophecy, speaking in tongues, and fasting to increase the effectiveness of our praying.

The focus of much of our praying is to be for the kingdom of God to come to earth, the lost to be found, and for the next generation to rise and serve God.

Such praying will be contested by Satan and his evil forces.

Consequently, God has given us powerful weapons to combat this.

This spiritual warfare is the reason that perseverance in prayer is essential.

Strike the Arrows

Elisha the prophet was ill and dying. So Jehoash, king of Israel, distressed at the thought of losing his spiritual father, visited him.[1]

At that time, the nation of Aram [2] was threatening Israel. To encourage the young king, Elisha said:

> Get a bow and some arrows. And the king did as he was told. Elisha told him, "Put your hand on the bow," and Elisha laid his own hands on the king's hands. Then he commanded, "Open that eastern window," and he opened it. Then he said, "Shoot!" So he shot an arrow. Elisha proclaimed, "This is the Lord's arrow, an arrow of victory over Aram, for you will completely conquer the Arameans at Aphek." [3]

This unusual act prophesied the great military victory that Jehoash would have over the Arameans. Firing an arrow out a window didn't make sense naturally, but in the spiritual realm, it was a statement of faith. Elisha then directed the king to do another prophetic act:

> Now pick up the other arrows and strike them against the ground. So the king picked them up and struck the ground three times. But the man of God was angry with him. "You should have struck

---

[1] See 2 Kings 13:14 where Jehoash calls Elisha "My father."
[2] Aram was an area that today includes Syria, south eastern Turkey, and parts of Lebanon and Iraq.
[3] 2 Kings 13:15-17

the ground five or six times!" he exclaimed. "Then you would have beaten Aram until it was entirely destroyed. Now you will be victorious only three times." [4]

Because the king did not persist, the victory against the Arameans would only be partial, rather than complete. Often, we settle for partial breakthroughs when God intends us to have complete breakthroughs. The key is persistence, even when it feels strange or when our logic fights us.

My first wife Jane suffered from terrible migraines that occurred frequently. After we married, I saw first-hand their debilitating effects. Forced to lie in a darkened room, gripped by nausea and severe pain, she was unable to eat or drink anything. This would last for two to three days, and had been a pattern since she was three years of age.

One day, in the middle of a new bout, I could not bear to see her in pain any longer. In fact, I became angry. While Jane lay ill in the bedroom, I prayed in an adjacent room. Jesus sometimes healed the sick by casting out the evil spirit causing the illness, so I asked God to set my wife free. Not every migraine is demonic in origin, but I sensed this one was. I then commanded the spirit to go in the name of Jesus.

After I prayed for a while, I asked Jane how she was. No change. I repeated this pattern three or four times. Still no change. Once more I prayed; once more I asked how she felt. "The pain is gone!" she replied.

---

[4]   2 Kings 13:18-19

The pain and nausea had left instantly, and she never had another migraine again. The Lord completely healed her. I often wonder what would have happened if I had given up too soon.

Prayer is the arrow of victory. Consistent striking of the arrow will see the kingdom of God break in upon our lives, families, churches, and nations. When you feel like giving up, strike the arrow again.

It's Time for Lions to Stand Up

A motivational speaker once told the story of a lion and an antelope. The sleeping lion, awakened by pangs of hunger, stirred itself and stood up. Catching the scent of an antelope herd, it began to stalk the group, focusing on a straggler. After pursuing the hapless animal, the lion caught and killed it. The speaker then asked the question, "When was it over for the antelope?" The answer was *the moment the lion stood up.*

"The righteous are as bold as a lion," declares the Bible.[5] God calls those made righteous through faith in Christ, lions. It's time for lions to awaken, stand up, and intercede for a world that needs heaven's interventions. When lions of faith stand up and roar in prayer, Christ also stands.

Today, Satan, the roaring lion,[6] is raging throughout the world, for he knows his time is short. Jesus, however, is called the Lion of Judah.[7] When he stands, it's over for the devil. The

---

5   Proverbs 28:1b (NIV)
6   See 1 Peter 5:8
7   See Revelation 5:5

Bible contains a number of references to Christ being seated at the right hand of the throne of his Father.[8] But there is a reference to him standing. When Stephen, the first martyr of the early church was being stoned to death, he exclaimed, "Look, I see the heavens opened and the Son of Man standing in the place of honour at God's right hand!" [9]

What made Jesus stand up? Was it because he was about to welcome Stephen into heaven? Was it because he was indignant at what was happening to his servant? Both are possibilities. But there is also a third reason. When Jesus stands, it's because he is about to take action against his enemies. "The enemy runs at the sound of your voice," declared the prophet Isaiah. "*When you stand up, the nations flee!*" [10] The psalmist cried, "Let God arise. Let His enemies be scattered." [11] The persistent intercession of God's people causes the Lord to stand up. And when he does so, he defeats all his enemies, no matter how intimidating they may look.[12]

The King Has Another Move

Many years ago, evangelist Billy Graham[13] told the following story in one of his meetings. Two men were visiting the Louvre in Paris. One of the men was an international chess champion, who

---

8   See Psalm 110:1, Ephesians 1:20, Colossians 3:1, Hebrews 12:2 and 1 Peter 3:22 for example.

9   Acts 7:56

10   Isaiah 33:3, emphasis mine.

11   Psalm 68:1a (NKJV)

12   Satan's forces are bound, and human enemies are either saved, or if not, eventually removed from their positions of influence.

13   Billy Graham, 1918-2018

179

was in the city for a chess tournament. During their tour of the famous art gallery, they came to a painting called *Checkmate*. The painting, by German artist Friedrich Retzsch, depicts a man (representing humanity) playing chess with the devil, while the angelic realm looks on. The devil smirks arrogantly because he has checkmated the man. In chess, when an opponent's piece can take your king off the board, and you can't stop it, it's checkmate, or game over. Or at least, that's what the artist meant to portray.

The chess champion stared at the chess board in the painting for a long time. Suddenly he stepped back, shocked. "It's wrong!" he exclaimed, "It's not checkmate. The king has another move!"

Jesus Christ, our king, always has another move.

When it looks like we are defeated, the king has another move.

When it looks like those we love are far away from God, the king has another move.

When it looks like the world is getting darker and darker, the king has another move.

When it looks like pandemics have shuttered the world, the king has another move.

When we engage in bold, persistent prayer, and loving mission, our king, the Lion of Judah, moves. Heaven opens, and his will is done on earth. As wonderful as this is, however, it is still not the greatest goal of prayer.

The Ultimate Destination

Prayer is not the final destination; it is a pathway to the end. While that end includes the kingdom of God breaking in upon earth, the salvation of the lost, and spiritual awakening, there is something even greater than these. The apostle Paul revealed it when he wrote:

> Do not be anxious about anything, but in every situation, by prayer and petition, with thanksgiving, present your requests to God. And the peace of God, which transcends all understanding, will guard your hearts and your minds in Christ Jesus. [14]

From a Roman prison, the apostle Paul wrote this to the Christians of his day, who faced terrible persecution and hostility from society. They are timeless words to people living in troubled times. Prayer, petition and thanksgiving are the means to bring our concerns for ourselves and our world to God.

Paul could have concluded with, "And God will answer your prayers." But he didn't. Instead, he emphasised that prayer enables us to enjoy the supernatural peace of God that guards our hearts, and keeps them in Christ. And that is the ultimate end of all prayer – that we are kept in Christ, so that no fear, worry, or world event can shake us from the perfect peace that only he gives.

---

[14]   Philippians 4:6-7 (NIV)

One day, when Jesus returns to earth, prayer will cease, for he is the culmination of all intercession and prayer. We will see him face to face and all the troubles of this present world will be swept away. Until that time, however, Jesus warned, "Here on earth you will have many trials and sorrows. But take heart, because I have overcome the world." [15]

Take heart. God our Father has given to us the ministry of prayer. It is the means to not only obtain answers to our and the world's problems, but to also guard our hearts and minds, and keep them in Christ. In Christ – that is the ultimate destination of this wonderful gift called prayer.

---

[15]   John 16:33

Appendix

PRAYING FOR REVIVAL AND SPIRITUAL AWAKENING

Many no longer pray for revival, as the global awakening we have long sought after, and interceded for, has not yet arrived. Yet God promises in his word that it will come. Around two and a half thousand years ago, the prophet Joel prophesied that God would pour out his Spirit on all people everywhere.[1] This was partially fulfilled on Pentecost Day, and through the Pentecostal and Charismatic movements of the twentieth century. There is a final, great fulfilment still to come. I hope to see it in my lifetime, but even if somehow I don't, I know that our prayers for a worldwide spiritual awakening will be seen by our children or grandchildren. But there is a condition.

---

[1]   See Joel 2:28-32

A Great Promise

It is one of the greatest promises in the Bible. Though given originally to the nation of Israel, it is a timeless promise for God's people in every generation. For the past few decades, the Holy Spirit has been emphasising it afresh:

> If my people, who are called by my name, will humble themselves and pray and seek my face and turn from their wicked ways, then I will hear from heaven, and I will forgive their sin and will heal their land. [2]

This is a promise to God's people, those saved through faith in Jesus. Most of the world's problems today can be traced back to its turning from God, or refusal to turn to him in the first place. God longs to heal the nations and is concerned for them.

A Vision

In 2017, when we were in the United Kingdom, Greta was woken suddenly in the middle of the night by the Holy Spirit. Instantly, she saw a vision of an enormous television screen. She writes:

> On the screen I saw video footage of all parts of the nation. I also heard the commentator and realised that it was Father speaking. This is what he said, "If my people, who are called by my name, will humble

---

[2]   2 Chronicles 7:14 (NIV)

themselves and pray and seek my face and turn from their wicked ways, then I will hear from heaven, and I will forgive their sin and will heal their land."

With each passing year since then, I have felt the Lord urging us more strongly to do this. He is ready and waiting to respond to the prayers of his people. In later visions, I saw Jesus as the Lion of Judah shining with glory, and roaring [3] over particular nations, including New Zealand. As he roared, fire and glory came out of his mouth for a great awakening and unprecedented harvest of salvation in those countries.[4]

In yet another vision, I saw why Jesus roared. He stood in the middle of Australia, and released a powerful roar that radiated to the shores of that continent. But I also saw, dotted in places all across the nation, people on their knees. They were obeying 2 Chronicles 7:14. Jesus' roar was in response to this. Though these visions involved specific nations, I believe that they apply to all nations.

The Bible says of Jesus, "When he saw the crowds, he had compassion on them, because they were harassed and helpless, like sheep without a shepherd." [5] The Lord hasn't changed.

---

[3] See Ezekiel 43:2 (NIV): "I saw the glory of the God of Israel coming from the east. His voice was like the roar of rushing waters, and the land was radiant with his glory."

[4] See Hosea 11:10b: "I, the Lord, will roar like a lion. And when I roar, my people will return trembling from the west." Though referring to Israel, this promise also applies to all of humanity that has strayed from God.

[5] Matthew 9:36 (NIV)

Today, he still has compassion for the harassed and helpless multitudes. God promises that if we seek him, he will heal the nations.

An Encounter

Near the end of writing this manuscript, I heard an American prophet share an encounter that he had had with the Lord. The Lord said to him:

> Do you know why there is so much trauma in your land? My people have not complied with 2 Chronicles 7:14. A few have humbled themselves; a few are praying for my kingdom to come and for my purposes. There is more prayer coming before me than ever in history, but most of it is for personal needs. Little of it is for the main prayer I gave you to pray: "Let my kingdom come, my will be done on earth as it is in heaven." [6]

Sobering words, but they confirm the contents of this book, especially the need to make the first part of the Lord's Prayer a priority. 2 Chronicles 7:14 also lists two other conditions: humbling ourselves (expressing our need of him, and fasting) and turning from known sin. Then God will listen.

Some may ask, "Why sit around waiting for revival? Let's reach the world now." And of course, they are right.

---

[6]   Rick Joyner, www.morningstartv.com/prophetic-perspective-current-events/morningstar-sos-afghanistan-crisis-pt-2, accessed 23/08/21

We are to combine prayer with mission – practical service, kind acts, and proclaiming the gospel – to demonstrate God's love to the world. We are to go as we pray, and pray as we go. However, we are now at a point in history where all our best efforts will not turn back the darkness that has permeated the world. We desperately need a sovereign move of God.

"The great need of the day," wrote American evangelist R. A. Torrey,[7] "is prayer, more prayer, and much prayer." This need has never been stronger today. The world needs an awakened Church. The world needs a Church on its knees practising 2 Chronicles 7:14 and the Lord's Prayer. If we do, the promised global outpouring of God's Spirit will come, and usher in the return of our Lord and King.

---

[7]   R A Torrey, 1856-1928.

In today's world, so many live with disappointment – never daring to dream or to have hope. In life, we all eventually encounter trouble. However, God promises, "I will transform the valley of trouble into a gateway of hope." In every valley of trouble or disappointment, there is a doorway of hope waiting to be found.

This book will help you discover that doorway. If you have lost hope, or want to develop a rugged, confident, biblical hope that is more than mere wishful thinking, then this book is for you.

"Full of gripping personal stories that made me weep and worship. I was encouraged and instructed by the great wisdom set down in these pages."
– John Dawson, President Emeritus, Youth With A Mission

Hope can be ordered from our website www.spiritlife.org.nz or any online bookstore (use the full title in your search).

Afterlife is the exciting sequel to *Hope*. Eventually death comes calling on us all. When it does, how can the living navigate through the agonising grief that envelops them at that time? What are the keys to experiencing life beyond bereavement?

And what of the dead - is there an afterlife for them? What is heaven like? What will our resurrection bodies be like? Scared of Judgment Day? You don't need to be if you follow the advice in this book. What will it be like to live in the new earth that God will create? In *Afterlife*, you will find the answers to these and many other questions.

"This brilliant book does not shy away from any aspect of truth and despite the solemnity of the subject matter, it is full of life and hope. I would highly recommend it to all."
– Tak Bhana, Senior Pastor, Church Unlimited, NZ

Afterlife can be ordered from our website www.spiritlife.org.nz or any online bookstore.

ABOUT DAVID AND GRETA

After graduating from Canterbury University, Christchurch, New Zealand, with a B.Sc. (Hons) degree in Chemistry, David became a secondary school teacher. Soon after, he and his first wife Jane pastored Elim churches in Picton and Wellington. He subsequently joined the pastoral staff of Auckland City Elim Church, but resigned three years later to care for Jane who had become disabled with multiple sclerosis.

In 2003 he and Jane commenced an itinerant ministry within New Zealand. Jane passed away in 2007. David later married Greta, and they have five sons between them.

After completing her B.Sc. (Physiotherapy) at the University of Cape Town, South Africa, Greta worked for some years at Groote Schuur Hospital before doing a post graduate Diploma in Teaching Physiotherapy. She lectured at UCT until the birth of her two sons. With her first husband Ron, she also studied extramurally with the Theological College of South Africa and they were involved in youth ministry at the Assemblies of God Churches in Cape Town. Greta also worked in children's ministry for many years.

In 1997, the family immigrated to Auckland, New Zealand where Ron passed away in early 2008. Greta ran her physiotherapy practice until late 2008 when she married David. Together with David, she helped found *SpiritLife Ministries*, and exercises a strong prophetic ministry in their travels.

David and Greta are currently based at Church Unlimited, a large, multicultural church in Auckland. They travel extensively both within New Zealand and overseas, inspiring people to have unwavering hope despite life's circumstances, equipping them to operate in the supernatural power of the Holy Spirit in daily life, and bringing prophetic encouragement to leadership teams.

To contact the author:

Email: davidp@spiritlife.org.nz

Website: www.spiritlife.org.nz

Facebook: www.facebook.com/SpiritlifeNZ

If you have enjoyed this book and found it helpful, why not order more copies for your family, friends, and pastor. Or you might like to sponsor copies to be given to pastors and leaders in developing nations, so they can teach their church members how to pray more effectively.